Connecting to Creativity

 Ten Keys to Unlocking
Your Creative Potential

Elizabeth W. Bergmann, M.A.

Elizabeth O. Colton, Ph.D.

CAPITAL BOOKS, INC. Sterling, Virginia

Capital Books, Inc.
22883 Quicksilver Drive
Sterling, Virginia 20166

ISBN 1-892123-09-6 (alk.paper)

Design and composition by Wilsted & Taylor Publishing Services

Printed in the United States of America on acid-free paper that meets
the American National Standards Institute Z39-48 Standard.

Attention, Organizations: Capital Books are available in quantity discounts with
bulk purchase for educational, business, or sales promotional use. For information,
please write to: Special Sales Department, Capital Books, P.O. Box 605, Herndon,
Virginia 20172-0605, or call Kathleen Hughes at 703-661-1511.

First Edition

10 9 8 7 6 5 4 3 2 1

CONTENTS

~~~~~~

PREFACE

~~~~~~

We, Liz and Liz, have both been fascinated by creativity since childhood, and we have each in our different lives been observing and analyzing the creative process in ourselves and others over our lifetimes. The process of creativity has been as interesting to each of us as the creative works we and others have produced.

We met in the early 1990s when we were both faculty members at Shenandoah University near Washington, D.C. Liz Bergmann was already there as Chair of the Dance Department when Liz Colton joined in 1991 to become Professor of Mass Communication and Journalism and Coordinator of the university's Mass Communications Program. Immediately upon introduction, we realized we were kindred spirits and became friends as we began talking about our mutually consuming interest in creativity and the creative process. Though in different schools of the university—the Conservatory and Arts and Sciences, respectively—we worked together as colleagues, always sharing ideas about teaching, growth, and creativity, and even exchanging our most creative students.

We discovered a mutual dream of founding an institute for creativity and determined to collaborate on this idea. We decided to begin by team-teaching a course in creativity, and our university awarded us interdisciplinary faculty-development grants to plan our course over the summer of 1997. We planned that each of us would present a lecture/workshop on creativity in our respective fields at the "Year 2000 Creative Arts Symposium" to be held that August in Trinidad and then, immediately afterwards, take a brief time there to plan our course for the next semester. In the meantime, however, Liz Bergmann decided to accept a new challenge and move to become Director of the Dance Program at Florida International University in Miami.

At first concerned that our plans for collaboration on a creativity course could not go forward as we would now be at separate universities, we decided that it was still important for us to proceed with our projects, to meet anyway in Trinidad, and while there see what we might do to continue and pursue our joint interest in the creative process. First of all, through the generous support of our respective universities, both Shenandoah and Florida International, we were each able to participate in the Creative Arts Symposium at the University of the West Indies outside Port of Spain in Trinidad. As we had hoped, this marvelous, multidisciplinary conference proved to be creatively inspirational, thanks to the innovative Caribbean organizers and creative participants from around the world.

At the conclusion of that inspiring symposium, we decided to spend the next three days together discussing and sharing our ideas about the creative process in the hopes of coming up with some plan for how we might work together teaching about creativity. Liz B., who had previously worked in Trinidad as a Fulbright Scholar, knew the perfect place for us to think creatively—a remote resort by the sea on Trinidad's northern coast facing toward the country's other island of Tobago. On the way, as we were driven through the lush, tropical countryside, we began planning how we would spend our time, hoping that we would be able to come up with some plan, though not sure exactly what we would be able to produce in this short time.

To our own amazement, by the time we arrived at this gloriously beautiful, tropical hideaway right on the beach, we realized that we were completely in sync with our ideas about the creative process. Instantly, we knew we should write a book together and should take the next three days in isolation from the outside world to plan it. Beginning from the moment we arrived at the rustic resort in Trinidad's Grande Rivière, we found ourselves on a rigorous schedule of outlining the book that you are now holding.

During our three days together by the sea—where our only distractions were the sounds of the waves, beach walks to see turtles hatching and entering the sea, swimming breaks in the deep green ocean, and eating fish and tropical fruits—our ideas for this book just tumbled out of us. It was exciting as we observed and participated in this amazing collaboration, agreeing completely on our ideas about the creative process, seeing the pattern unfolding in front of us as we talked and wrote and shared our visions, experiences, and plans.

We believe that if we had not experienced this together, this unique artistic and intellectual collaboration, we might have questioned the process that we are here outlining and describing. But, instead, since we both corroborated the exact steps leading to the moment of creation, we realized that this process was not, is not, a mystery. Rather, as we emphasize here in our finished book, the creative process always follows a very definite pattern, a sequence of steps, no matter how compressed or expanded any one step might be at any one point for different individuals and projects. We were thrilled with our discovery, and there, overlooking the sea on Trinidad's remote northern coast, we committed ourselves to writing and eventually publishing this book.

From then on, every time we met to work on *Connecting to Creativity*, whether in Florida or Virginia or on long-distance telephone calls and Internet links between far-flung points of the globe, we always continued to be amazed at our incredible collaboration in which together we discussed, conceptualized, composed, and wrote one page, one chapter after another, even joint sentences. Later, when our publisher, Kathleen P. Hughes, intending to be helpful, suggested that we might want to divide up the book and each of us write different chapters, we emphatically declined because we knew that we were able to work and write completely as a creative team. Remarkably, even our anecdotes, which we initially wrote as individual contributions, were often so similar, even sometimes the same, that we have consolidated some of them into unified examples. This further discovery of the amazing similarity of our lifetime experiences with the creative process, though in different fields, basically proves the validity of the ideas for "connecting to creativity" we put forth in this book.

We are very proud and thrilled, therefore, to state that this book, while based on our individually experienced understanding, has been a totally joint effort, every word and every paragraph, written together during intensely creative work sessions. The entire experience has been extremely stimulating and exciting and is evidence every step of the way for the program we set forth here. We have proof now from both our individual and collaborative experiences that these are the "ten keys to unlocking your creative potential." Now we want to share our ideas with YOU.

—*Liz Bergmann and Liz Colton*

ACKNOWLEDGMENTS

~~~~~~

My family and friends have always been great sources of love and encouragement for my creative visions, adventures, and independence. I am very grateful to all of them as I continue to strive to live a creative life. Both my mother and my father, Marie and Henry Colton, themselves creative in how they have lived, encouraged my creative endeavors from early childhood—one project after another—and they never once said I should not try a new idea. My grandmothers, Sadie Watters and Elizabeth Colton, each in her own way, urged me to follow independent, creative paths. My sisters, Marie and Sarah, and my brother, Walter, always remain great sources of strength and spiritual support. And now I am appreciative of their children, my nieces and nephews, for sharing their creative endeavors. Likewise, I thank my co-author, Liz Bergmann, for carrying on this wonderful dialogue about creativity that led to our book.

—*Elizabeth Colton*

My artistic family, as far back as I can remember, put making art and expressing oneself in my genes and valued the power and excitement of the creative process. My grandfather, Albert Winfield, and my mother, Frances Weil, were both artists and both encouraged my freedom of spirit and adventure in my creative journey. My daughter, Sasha, who is my constant inspiration, is a powerful artist who shares her visions with me and the world; and my son-in-law, Benyamin Bergmann Lichtenstein, has an incisive mind and brilliance that always pushes me into new places. I thank my son,

~ Acknowledgments

Christopher, for his great power to love, which he infuses in all of his life, and I appreciate him for his music which he carries in his heart. My Father, Ervin Weil, made possible all of my education with so many great people. I thank my co-author, Liz Colton, with whom I have shared an incredible creative experience.

—*Elizabeth Bergmann*

We thank Kathleen Hughes, our editor and publisher, who believes in our ideas. We also acknowledge with much gratitude those in Trinidad who contributed to the initial realization of this work—the University of the West Indies and its inspiring 1997 Creative Arts Education Symposium, Pierro Guerrini for providing us with the perfect space for creative work at his Grande Rivière hideaway on the north coast, and Mathilde Demy of Martinique who observed us at work in Trinidad and encouraged our first plan for this book. We are grateful to Shenandoah University and Florida International University for supporting our traveling to and participating in the inspirational conference in Trinidad. We are also very appreciative of Michele Peters for her immediate excitement and encouragement upon learning about our book and for her Miami friends, John Martin and Elayne Krakauer, all three of whom gave us their time and shared their special experiences and ideas. More than we can enumerate, we honor our teachers, our students, and our friends, all who have supported, listened, prodded, and encouraged us, and held our hands while we individually pursued the amazing internal journeys we have already taken and must continue to follow in order to be the expressive persons we are.

—*Liz & Liz*

~~~~~~~~~~~~~~~~~~~~~~~~~~~~~~~~~~~~

How Can You Become Your Most Creative Self?

W hat is creativity?

Creativity is the energy to transform. It is the expression of a person's uniqueness. It is the expression of YOUR uniqueness—to be who you are in all ways. The ability to create exists in everyone. Manifesting your uniqueness is the greatest fulfillment you can have in your life.

Creativity is the expression of the self.
Creativity is imagination.
Creativity is innovation.
Creativity is inspiration.
Creativity is the leap beyond the data, going beyond the known.
Creativity is the totality of everything you are and can be.
Creativity requires you to be daring, to take risks.
Creativity requires that you be attentive to your inner urges.
Creativity is the ultimate control over your life.
Creativity is joyful, fun, playful.
Creativity is also the most satisfying of all experiences.
Creativity exists in everyone.
Creativity is available to everyone.

"Creativity" and "creative" come from the active verb "to create." According to *Webster's Encyclopedic Unabridged Dictionary of the*

English Language, "creativity" is both the state or quality of being creative and the creative ability or process. "Creative" describes the quality or power of creating, or something resulting from originality of thought or expression, or being originative, productive. And "creation" can be the act of creating, producing, or causing to exist, or the fact of being created. In a theological sense, the Creation is the original bringing into existence of the universe by God. More generally, creation is that which is or has been created; the world; the universe; creatures collectively; and an original product of the mind, an imaginative artistic work.

Creativity is like unseen electricity and energy linking us to the rest of the universe. Creativity in ourselves appears to reveal that we are in some kind of cosmic link with all of creation. We are both receiver and transmitter, and we must open ourselves up to allow the process of creativity to flow.

~ *When I was a young girl, between nine and ten years old, I used to spend hours alone in my room, sometimes being banished there as punishment and other times just because I wanted to be by myself and write. For whatever reason I was there, it was then that I would write stories, music, plays, poems, even a little novel, articles for my newspapers. Often I played with my paper dolls and let them act out my dramas. Sometimes I would get so deep into my creative activities that I would begin trying to imagine "infinity" and the ends of the universe. Then, almost in a trance, I would imagine merging with the universe and whatever infinity was. I remember that it was both an exciting and frightening experience but one I often sought to enter whenever I went deeply into my creative projects. (L.C.)*

~ *When I was eight years old, my favorite aunt died. I had no one to counsel me or interpret for me this powerful experience and my feelings of great loss. I began to write short stories about where I thought she had gone and how much I missed her. I used to lie on my back in the yard and imagine seeing her in the cloud formations above. I missed her so much and found that I could connect with some dream of her through my imaginings and my writings.* (L.B.)

All creative artists, inventors, and many great scientists allude to this experience of creation as if the creative work comes through them from some other source, in some mysterious and almost magical way. But, most importantly, this experience is not limited only to artists or to those people society calls geniuses. The creative process is an experience available to all people who have a willingness and a desire to live a fully expressed life in whatever endeavors they pursue. *Connecting to Creativity* demystifies without taking away the beauty and excitement of the process. Through a step-by-step description of the process that takes place in every complete act of creative endeavor, this book reveals the keys to tapping into your own creative potential.

Why do you need creativity? Living more creatively in every way can bring untold benefits to every aspect of your existence— to your work, to your play, to your relationships, to your whole life. Especially now during the technological revolution that is transforming our lives, our entire world economy and social order, more people than ever have the freedom to be as creative as they can and to take their ideas and talents out into the global marketplace or to take time off to enrich their souls with creative works. At this moment of millennial change, creativity is open to you for your own creative expression in a myriad of ways never before imagined possible. *Connecting to Creativity* tells you exactly how to enter and harness the creative process in your life.

YOU AND YOUR CREATIVITY

Have you ever thought there was something deep down that you wanted to express or to change in your life and you have not been able to tap into it?

Have you wanted to create beauty and to share it with the rest of the world?

And have you believed that the expression you've always wanted to bring out would be unique to you alone?

If your answer to any of the above is yes, then this book is for you. The problem is how to tap into this inner creativity.

~ I keep having this strong sense that I am a creative person. But I cannot figure out how to do it, what to do. I want to do something about it. I want to open up and let myself be creative about the way I live. What I need is help right now to get started. (M.P.)

~ I always knew I was creative. I now know I have been an artist all my life. I never felt as if I truly fit in. I tried to conform, but everything felt uncomfortable. I didn't know how to be like everyone else. I only knew how to be me. Growing up was a terrible time for me, and it took many years to find myself again, but I never stopped dancing. I think that kept me as sane as I was, given that I found the world very perplexing and could not understand where I fit into it. As a kid, I would come home from school at lunchtime and dance my lunch hour away. Every night I provided the family entertainment, putting on costumes and dancing my heart out. What would I have done as a child without the outlets of dancing and writing and dreaming? Fortunately, my childhood was before the era of television, which might have mesmerized me away from my feelings. I feel lucky that I grew up freely, with lots of access to nature, to very few planned activities. I had time to explore my feelings and find ways to express the emotions that were swirling inside me. (L.B.)

~ For some reason I've never understood, from the very moment I began to learn to write, I knew that I wanted to be a writer. Of course, there were a lot of other things I thought I wanted to do, and, perhaps, I might have. Certainly, as a child, I tried many activities and had many dreams, but it's the idea of being a writer that has stayed with me ever since I was very young.

I still feel I have something, many things, very important to say and write, and it's been a lifetime, constant endeavor to tap into my creativity. (L.C.)

YOU CAN BE THE CREATIVE PERSON
YOU WANT TO BE

Say to yourself, "I CAN BE THE CREATIVE PERSON I WANT TO BE."

That is what *Connecting to Creativity* reveals to you in ten exciting and enjoyable, yet challenging steps—giving you the keys to unlocking your own creative potential. It describes the process for releasing the creative genius within you and unlocking the creative powers that we believe exist in every person.

The creative process can be used in all aspects of your life. This book reveals the steps in this process, demonstrating that it is not elusive, but available to all people willing to take the keys and unlock the doors to their own creative potential.

Connecting to Creativity can be used by people in all walks of life and around the world. While many books on creativity address the issue only for artists or for the recognizably talented, this one is directed not only to this group but also, and importantly, to every one of us.

Why this book when there are so many others out there talking about creativity? This book actually describes the process for releasing the creative genius within each person, unraveling the age-old mystery of what has appeared to be an elusive phenomenon. Whether you are an artist, an aspiring artist, a businessperson, a teacher, a parent, or anyone else desiring to enhance the quality of your life, this book will help you to release and shape your creativity. It is designed for all people—because the potential for creativity exists in everyone.

The amazing discovery that we have made is that there are ten distinct stages in the creative process. This book describes this universal, step-by-step process that successful artists, entrepreneurs, dealmakers, designers, inventors, and all creative persons, whether they are aware of it or not, use in their lives to unlock their creativity. For most people who apply their creativity in their daily lives and work, this process is unconscious. While the ultimate work, the final product, is quite different for an entrepreneur, an artist, or a scientist, the steps of the process are the same to reach the diverse goals of a successful business, a creative deal, an invention, a work of art, a marketing plan, a scientific discovery. This book presents an easy-to-read program that makes these secrets accessible, giving everyone the opportunity to experience and share their own creative genius.

If followed, this remarkable pathway to creativity can lead to more abundant and fulfilling lives for everyone. Inspiration from the muse will be available to all those who learn how to summon it by following the process described here. It can help you generate the passion and originality to live a very special and meaningful life. The techniques taught here can be applied in all aspects of your life, including even your relationships with other people.

In discovering your own creative powers, you will be reaching into the essential core of your being. Tapping into your creative potential is a very personal, intimate, and sacred act. Getting in touch with your own creativity will inform you about your life's journey and help you find meaning in your own life's experiences. It is about committing to self-knowledge through your own creative source and being willing—and able—to share your discoveries with others in a creative work. It is about looking at who you really are and expressing that essence. No one can do this for you. In this entire process, you will be building a deep understanding of and relationship with yourself.

Life is a complex puzzle, and our creative experiences help us to unravel the mysteries of our lives. As a creative person, YOU will develop an inner knowing and an inner strength. You will learn to cherish and protect your creative endeavors the rest of your life because they represent you.

Your creativity and all your creations are YOU.

Connecting to Creativity will change forever the way you think about your own access to creativity and the role it can play in your life.

~~~~~~~~~~~~~~~~~~~~~~~~~~~~~~~~~~~~~~~

Getting Started on the Creative Process

Expressing part of yourself through the creative process is one of the most fulfilling experiences of life. Not only can it give you some of your most ecstatic moments, but it can also be vital to a healthy and fulfilled life. Finding a means of expressing your unique self is as important to your well-being as food, having a roof over your head, and intimate relationships.

THE JOYS OF CREATIVITY

The act of creating is just as urgent as birthing a child. Just as you can't hold back the birth of a baby without risking the life of the mother, you can't hold back your creative expression without the risk of endangering your own health. Whatever the trials, whatever the pitfalls, there is no experience on this earth like letting your creativity flow.

Everyone has the potential to be creative. The problem for many is that we do not know how to tap into this inner creativity. The process has seemed to be locked behind closed doors as a secret open only to a very few. In many cultures, human beings who do not bring out and share their unique gifts are viewed as not participating fully in their community. Everyone should express their uniqueness through creativity.

If you do not share your gifts, your own unique form of creativity, no one else can do it for you. This book unlocks the mysteries of the creative process, revealing that it is not elusive but available to all people willing to take the keys and unlock the doors to this process.

It is important to note, however, that this book is not about turning everyone into an artist. It is about how everyone can tap into her and his creative potential in a personal way. Here we are simply offering a proven approach to becoming a more creative being. This book answers the question "How am I going to do it—be a more creative person?"

FIRST STEPS: ACKNOWLEDGMENT AND INTENTION

The first important requirement to starting the creative process is twofold:

1. Knowing that you do have this potential for creativity, knowing deep down there's something expressive, creative, that needs to come out of you, and then,
2. Committing yourself to do something about it, demonstrating a willingness to express your creative potential.

ACTION 1: State out loud to yourself that you acknowledge you do have creative potential and that you intend to do something about bringing it out. Then put in writing your acknowledgment and your intention.

ASSESSING YOUR CREATIVITY

The fact that you picked up this book in the first place shows that you believe you have creative potential. In order to explore further what this means—that YOU do have great creative potential and can bring it out to the world, please take the following test.

Creativity Potential Test	YES	NO
Do you feel that there is more to you than you are expressing?	☒	☐
Are there things inside you pressing to come out?	☒	☐
Do you want to become a more fully expressed human being?	☒	☐
Have you ever had a thought or an idea that you felt was deep down inside you that you needed to express?	☒	☐
Have you ever wanted to change something in your life in order to live more expressively?	☒	☐
Have you ever wanted to create beauty?	☒	☐
Have you ever wanted to share something special of yourself with the rest of the world?	☒	☐
Do you have ideas for creative projects but don't know how to express them?	☒	☐

If your answer to any one of the above is yes, then you have clearly demonstrated that Y O U have creative potential.

Do you realize that the expression you want to bring out is unique to you alone, that only you can bring it out from deep down inside you, and that only you can manifest what is uniquely, creatively yours?

Do you realize that what you express might help others realize a concept of beauty?

ASSESSING YOUR WILLINGNESS TO BE CREATIVE

Now that you recognize your creative potential, do you intend to develop and pursue these gifts?

Connecting to Creativity ~

Do you have the willingness and the discipline to follow your call to creativity? Once you have personally acknowledged your creative potential and announced your intention to yourself, to move forward toward the goal of living up to your creative potential, the first thing you must now be willing to do is to make a commitment to the actions in the following test. Stating your willingness to pursue your gifts is the critical next step in the process.

~~~~~~

Creativity Willingness—The "Willings" Test	YES	NO
Are you willing to make a commitment to fulfill your creative potential and do all that will be necessary, including spending time alone and exercising self-discipline?	■	☐
Are you willing to make a clearing for your creative space?	■	☐
Are you willing to let your creativity germinate—stare into space and appear to be doing nothing?	■	☐
Are you willing to find your creative direction?	■	☐
Are you willing to get your ideas out of your head and into a form?	■	☐
Are you willing to create the work?	■	☐
Are you willing to share your creation?	■	☐
And, after you've created your creation, are you willing to begin again?	■	☐

~~~~~~

If you've answered yes to most of the above, you are ready to begin. If you've not been able to respond positively to these, then we suggest you go to the section about "Blocks" on page 17. All of the above can now become the "Willings" in your creative life.

WHAT YOU NEED TO GET STARTED

To pursue your creative potential, you must be willing to make a serious commitment to dedicate a portion of your life to the development of your own creativity. To that end, you must be willing to commit yourself to the following seven critical elements from the start and carry them with you through the whole process:

1. You must have a journal and be willing to write/jot/ sketch in it regularly.

2. You must create time alone and be willing to dedicate yourself to it regularly.

3. You must be willing to struggle to banish inner and outer criticism.

4. You must be willing to develop your self.

5. You must be willing to create and use affirmations in order to change any belief systems that are in the way of your goals.

6. You must be willing to pay attention to inner and outer messages all the time—not only during your specified creative time but also during your breaks.

7. You must be willing to exert—develop and maintain— inner discipline.

JOURNALING: THE BOOK
THAT NEVER LEAVES YOUR SIDE

Keeping some kind of journal—a regular record of your thoughts, ideas, visions—is another vital component of beginning to live a creative life. It gives you a means of capturing your ideas for current or later use. It also provides a private outlet for expression of your daily adventures and struggles and achievements as you move along your very own unique, creative path.

To do this, you need to buy a special, beautiful journal and a special pen/pencil for writing down your ideas. Having such a special journal will encourage you to keep these valuable notes of your life. This book should never leave your side. Take it everywhere you go. Take it with you to work. Keep it on your bedside table.

~ *My journal is always with me. The purchase of my journal has always been a special activity because I treasure these little books of my life and thoughts. Writing daily in a journal, a diary, a notebook, has been a part of my life for long before it became fashionable to do so. Always thinking of myself as a writer, I have been keeping journals of my life from early childhood. It's always amazing to me to go back, from time to time, and read over my journals from years past. Sometimes it seems I'm still writing about the same old problems, the same goals I'm not attaining. At other times, though, I recognize the growth. There are times, too, when I re-discover forgotten dreams and enjoy the opportunity to re-ponder them. When I was a young adult and more inhibited than as a child or now as a more mature person, I was often guarded in what I wrote in my journals, or at least I might write in code. At one point, though, in my early 30s, I decided to write absolutely honestly, whatever I was thinking, whatever I was feeling, whatever was happening in my life. The entire, regular, usually daily process of writing in my journals, diaries, is both a meditation and a catharsis. It is an essential part of my life.* (L.C.)

If "journaling" is new to you, begin by writing in your journal at least fifteen minutes a day. Let anything come that wants to flow out—from your head through your writing instrument into the journal. Sometimes this is called automatic writing. Do not edit it or be critical of what comes. This is a private, non-shared activity. So enjoy total freedom in expressing your thoughts, ideas, any mental and emotional rumblings and ramblings.

~ *I had written a bit in my life, but I had never "journaled" (regularly kept a journal of my life and feelings and ideas). At 52 years of age, after my divorce and after having taken a job on the East Coast, I set out upon my exodus from California to start a new life. I stopped in Tucson to spend the first night of my journey with a very dear friend, and the next morning as I was leaving, Anna gave me a beautiful blank journal. Handing it to me, she said, "You are going on an amazing journey. You must keep a record of your adventures and your changes." And from that day forward, I began journaling my new life, writing my poems and my dreams and my dances as I went along the way. I now have over 40 journals filled with my life, my passions, and my dreams of future projects.* (L.B.)

ACTION 2: Choose a writing book for your special journal. Find one from among your own collection of notebooks, or purchase one that is unusual and enticing to you, or even make one. Begin to keep your own journal of your ideas, thoughts, feelings, experiences, any kinds of notations that are important to you.

BEING ALONE: TAKE ME AND MYSELF AWAY TOGETHER—I ALL ALONE

To begin to realize your creative potential, you must be willing to spend a great amount of time alone. Contemporary culture with its many distractions lures us away from spending quality time alone. It is during this time by ourselves when we can begin to receive inner knowings and messages about who we are and urges to be expressive. Regular and substantial periods of alone time are vital to cultivating our creativity. This is the beginning of research and observation of your creative self.

~ I have found out that I cannot live without the proper amount of solitude. I must be alone a lot. It is in my alone time that I flow with the universal energy, where I feel connected to all that is. From this time with my muse— when I am all alone with myself—I reach into the fountain of eternity,

knowing truly that I am a "forever-being," journeying with great passion and fervor on this earth for a short while. My life takes on meaning, and I am at peace. (L.B.)

Being alone can be accomplished in all kinds of ways—by taking a daily silent walk, or walking on a treadmill with nothing but your thoughts, swimming, sitting by a body of water, gardening, cleaning your house, puttering alone in your house without television, or being alone in a special part of your house.

~ *Being able to go off and be alone has always been a necessary ingredient of my life. But it's only been in recent years, as I've grown older, that I have firmly acknowledged to myself how absolutely essential taking time to be alone is for my peace of mind and for developing and inspiring my creativity. Now, no matter where I am, no matter what work I'm doing, no matter what my living situation, I make every effort to be alone for some time during the day. I now find myself throughout the day disappearing from society for brief periods to be alone, whether it's sitting all by myself in a restaurant or taking a walk or even going and sitting quietly in a restroom of some building, if that is all that's available. Such moments, however long or short, allow me to catch my breath, re-establish myself, plan my next steps, let my creative energy re-fill and emerge.* (L.C.)

Being a creative person in any field of work requires taking time out frequently to be alone and allow yourself to become rejuvenated.

~ *Because I'm such a sociable person and have a job overseeing lots of people, paying attention to lots of details—basically running a huge operation—most people never think of me as being alone. But I have to take lots of time to be alone whenever I'm away from work in order to be the best and most creative administrator and manager of people. I think it's my solitude that gives me the strength to do all my very sociable, people- and task-oriented work.* (S.C.)

ALONE ACTIVITIES

In this quality alone time, you will want to do only the following:

Nothing.
Listen to your inner voices.
Dream, vision, let your imagination run wild.
Capture on paper the ideas that come to you during this
    alone time.

~~~~~~~~~~~~~~~~~~~~~~~~~~~~~~~~~~~~

For Your Time Alone

DO	DON'T
Sit and do nothing	Allow outside distractions
Imagine	Listen to music or play
Sing	computer games
Dream	Use your Walkman or watch TV
Meditate	Do aerobics
Listen to the birds	Talk to friends
Write from your heart	E-mail friends
Dance alone creatively	Listen to the radio
Play an instrument alone	Read

Add your own favorite ways to spend your alone time.

~~~~~~~~~~~~~~~~~~~~~~~~~~~~~~~~~~~~

ACTION 3: Begin your creative actions by observing, becoming mindful of this quality time with yourself. Notice how much time you spend alone in a day— without television, without the Internet, without music, without conversation, without engaging in busywork. During this time of solitude, however, you may engage in meditation, creative dancing, wandering around the house or garden, taking a walk, writing in your journal from your heart. Try different places for spending your alone time until you find the most satisfying places for you.

ACTION 4: Begin to record in your journal the times you spend alone. Take notice of where you are and what goes on in your mind when you are alone, doing nothing. Write about it or make sketches in your journal.

OVERCOMING OBSTACLES AND BLOCKS TO YOUR CREATIVITY

Chase away your fears. As you begin to move toward realizing your creative potential, you must be prepared to overcome the tests and distractions, all your inhibitions and excuses, that will immediately and constantly appear in your way. This will occur throughout the process. You will have to be especially prepared to deal with both external and internal critics that will come at you from every direction seeking to knock you off your path and even trying to halt your progress.

Whether you are living alone, or with another person, or in a family, you will be assaulted by many self-imposed and externally imposed reasons telling you that you should not spend time alone. If you live alone already, you may feel that you constantly have to seek out company in order not to be labeled a recluse. Or, even if it does not bother you to be alone, you may still have to persuade your friends to appreciate your need to cut yourself off from their society for periods of time to do your thing. Or, if you live with other people, you may have to persuade them about the importance to you of having time alone to be creative. A few people have spouses and companions who understand and make every effort to give you that space. Most people, though, have to struggle to get that time and space to be alone with their creativity.

~ *I couldn't sleep all night. It was as though some spirit inside me couldn't rest. I remember when I was married, and I had these bursts of energy. I wanted to climb out of bed and go at it, to be creative. Instead, I would lie awake, sleeplessly, not wanting to disturb my mate. For years, I had wanted to ask for a room of my own, a place that was only mine, where I could work or sleep when the spirit so moved me. But I was in a conventional marriage with a conventional guy, and I thought that my desires would not be understood. Unwilling to talk about what I needed in this way, I never got that room. Eventually I left the marriage, probably more to get a room of my own than for many other reasons. How foolish now that I look back that I could not request this very simple need of mine.* (L.B.)

ACTION 5: List and discuss in your journal all the obstacles, internal and external excuses, that you use to try to prevent yourself from moving forward with your creativity.

~ *I find that many people don't know how to talk to creative persons about their work. Sometimes this is a very upsetting realization for creative people. But once you realize it, then you can just overlook the problem and ignore others' lack of understanding about your own needs to be a creative person.* (E.K.)

ACKNOWLEDGING YOUR OWN LIST OF EXCUSES
~~~~~~~~~~~~~~~~~~~~~~~~~~~~~~~~~~~~~~~

How many of these excuses apply to you?

	YES	NO
I am afraid of really letting my creativity come out.	■	☐
I am afraid of the unknown.	■	☐
I am afraid of being alone for long.	☐	■
I am afraid of unleashing my creative powers.	■	☐
I fear the voice of the critical parent inside me who says, "You can't ever do anything worthwhile."	■	☐

How many of these excuses apply to you? (continued)   YES   NO

	YES	NO
I'm no good.	☐	☒
All my ideas are boring.	☒	☐
I can't complete anything.	☐	☒
Nobody would be interested in what I have to say or do anyway.	☒	☐
My job is too demanding.	☒	☐
I have too many demands from my children.	☐	☒
I have too many responsibilities to others.	☒	☐
I want a guarantee that I will succeed.	☐	☒
I have to have everything in place before I start.	☒	☐
I have to know that I have enough money to support myself.	☐	☒
I have a sick mother/friend/spouse/child to care for.	☐	☒
I'm too tired.	☐	☒
I have no time.	☒	☐
I want to watch my favorite television show.	☐	☒
I have to answer my e-mail.	☐	☒
My social life is too active.	☐	☒
It would be too selfish.	☐	☒
There are too many demands on my life already.	☒	☐
My husband/wife/lover/partner wants me available all the time.	☐	☒

Now add any other excuse that you have allowed to block your own efforts to reach your creative potential.

It won't be good enough
I want to be sure what will happen
People won't understand or like it/me.

~~~~~~~~~~~~~~~~~~~~~~~~~~~~~~~~~~~~~

USING AFFIRMATIONS

You are your beliefs. Affirmations are personal statements, images, of your wishes and desires. They are used to push yourself forward toward achieving what you wish to do in your life. Some people keep affirmations repetitively written out and posted in many places where they will see them throughout the day. Many people say their affirmations to themselves hourly. These methods have proven to be very successful.

~ *It took a long time before I finally realized that I wanted to do something creative with my life. But, in order to do that at such a late date (or so it seemed), I knew I would have to make radical changes in my life. The problem of being creative for me was very much mixed in with my fear of financial problems. I had to look inside myself to recognize all the negativity tapes that kept playing, and then I had to figure out how to play over them—I don't believe you can ever fully erase them—but play over them with new positive, encouraging tapes. So what I did was first of all begin to write out affirmations, like "I will change," "I can change," "I can live a creative life," and I pasted these affirmation notes all over my house—on mirrors, on doors, on the refrigerator. And, to my amazement, what I wrote in my affirmations began to become real in my life.* (J.M.)

~ *When I decided to change my life and begin again to live more creatively, I put affirming statements and pictures everywhere. Within a few years, I had begun to achieve all that I set out to do about moving into newly creative directions, playing again with paper, wood, and clay, and eventually leaving my work as a longtime administrator. To my great surprise and joy, I even realized my dream of being in the inspiring presence of the Dalai Lama after pinning a picture of him onto my refrigerator.* (E.N.)

~ *Often I have dreams with words of instruction that become affirmations for me. For example, when I was trying to finish a major creative project,*

and I kept getting thrown off course, I had a dream with the ⌐
else matters!" On waking, I remembered the words from
wrote them down on note-cards that I then placed all over
mind myself that I must not get distracted—by anyone or anything—from
my important work. I have an image in my mind of these kinds of affirma-
tions having the same kind of power in warding off negative, destructive
forces and distractions as we were told symbols like the sign of the cross were
thought to have against vampires or the color blue against the evil eye.
(L.C.)

To stand up for yourself and to prove to yourself that you have a unique expression to share, you might wish to repeat the following affirmation to yourself—or make one up that best fits you. Whatever affirmation you choose to use, keep it in the forefront of your mind at all times.

ACTION 6: Begin saying the following affirmation (or your own) to yourself:

I am unique, and
　　No one else can think what I think
　　Dream what I dream
　　Sing what I sing
　　Say what I say
　　Create what I create.

You may want to put copies of this affirmation around your own house or place of work, your office, your studio—to keep reminding yourself of your creative self.

SELFING

Who is most important in your life anyway?

Once you decide and begin to spend significant amounts of time alone in order to pursue your creative potential, you may be accused of being selfish by other people. Instead, develop the concept of "SELFING." No longer is it appropriate to consider it as a selfish act to dedicate quality time to yourself in order to develop your unique gifts. A better construct, or equation, is that you are selfing—you are preparing to bring out your unique gifts to the world.

~ *It was a time in my life when I felt I had to make some radical changes and to begin to do some completely different, creative work, but the problem initially was that I did not know what to do. And, worse, because of my very time-consuming job at the time, I seemed to have no time for myself to think about what to do next. My current income-producing job was very people-oriented, and there were many demands upon me from many different people. I finally realized that I had to set aside weekly periods of time to be alone as long as possible throughout the day, in order, over a long period of time, to try to figure out the next direction for my life. I decided to devote most of every Sunday to being only with myself. Then my friends became annoyed that I would not make time for them on weekends. It was difficult, but I stuck to my plan. And I am glad because it was then that new ideas came to me, and I finally found my new direction.* (E.W.)

It is important also that you realize that in selfing, you will need the following:

ENDURANCE

SELF-DISCIPLINE

HIGH ENERGY

Selfing is your obligation to be all you can be for yourself, society, and all the people around you.

Connecting to Creativity ~

SELFING INVENTORY

~~~~~~

By now you have spent some time selfing. The next step is for you
to take a preliminary inventory of who you are and what blocks are
preventing you from living as creatively as possible.

                                                        YES NO

Are you willing to manipulate your excuse-list to find
    valuable time for yourself?   ☒   ☐
Have you been successful in promoting your own selfing
    in the past?   ☐   ☒
Can you clear time for your selfing endeavor?   ☒   ☐
Are you filling your life with activities that become
    excuses because basically you are afraid of being alone
    or afraid that you cannot be all that you wish to be?   ☒   ☐

~~~~~~

~ *I was sitting on the beach, early in the morning. The gulls were searching
the deposits left on the beach from the night's activity. They were sunning
themselves and airing their wings. I thought, "Animals and birds take care
of themselves all day long. That is their most important function—sleeping
and eating and cleaning themselves as needed. They relate, mate, and care
for their young. But, primarily, I notice that they take care of themselves. If
they don't, they won't survive. Not taking care of themselves first really
makes them unable to care for anything else. If they don't take care of themselves, they will die." How did we as humans forget this important lesson?
And why do we ostracize those humans who do take care of themselves first,
knowing that they must do so in order to be valuable to themselves and to
others?* (L.B.)

ACTION 7: Write about what selfing would mean in your life. List what activities and changes you would need to make in order to fulfill your need for selfing.

If you notice after taking this selfing inventory that you're still not able to take time for yourself, then try making changes in small increments over a period of days or even weeks to work yourself into the habit of selfing.

A SUPPORT SYSTEM AND A FRIEND TO HOLD YOU TO IT

You need to create very supportive environments for yourself in order to do your creative work. Some people find it helpful to ask a trusted friend to hold them accountable and help them stick with their commitments to themselves. This does not mean that you should share your ideas, but only that you should tell your friend you are taking steps to pursue your creative potential.

This kind of support can be as simple as a phone call stating that you are beginning an activity and expressing your intentions and how long you plan to do something. Then you will want to check in to report that you've made progress or need encouragement to continue and then, finally, to report your accomplishments at the end. Although this support is helpful, it may also bring up blocks. But do not be frightened off.

ACTION 8: Ask a friend to help you keep your commitment. This is the critical point at which you express your intention to yourself and to the rest of the world around you. This is when you state to yourself first and then to others your willingness to try to discover your uniqueness and to express your creative potential by being alone sometime in every day. Choose someone you can trust to be supportive to confide your intention to.

TAKING BREAKS

Some of your best ideas come when you're doing
It is very important that throughout this process yo
to take breaks. Be alert to the fact that once you are in this creative
process, you will discover that many of your best ideas will come
when you are doing something else, like playing a game or sport,
or driving in your car, or even when you are brushing your teeth or
showering. Einstein himself noticed that many of his most brilliant
ideas came when he was shaving.

It is critical that you quickly record such ideas that come during
your breaks. One suggestion is to keep a tape recorder with you in
your car. And, of course, try to keep your journal or at least a note-
pad with you wherever you go so that later, when you are concentrating on being in your creative time, you will not forget the brilliant ideas you have had during your break.

Remember that you are the only one who can share your unique
gifts with the world. Only you can manifest what is uniquely creative in yourself.

ARE YOU NOW READY TO PROCEED?

~~~~~~~~~~~~~~~~~~~~~~~~~~~~~~~~~~~~~~~

If you can answer these questions, you are ready . . .   YES NO

Have you begun your journey to reach your creative
   potential?   ☐   ☐
Do you know that deep down there's something
   expressive, creative, that needs to come out of you?   ☐   ☐
Do you intend to do something about it?   ☐   ☐
Do you now acknowledge that you do have this potential
   for creativity?   ☐   ☐

if you can answer these questions, you are ready . . .
    (continued)   YES NO

Have you stated to yourself, and perhaps to others, your
    willingness to try and express your creative potential?   ☐   ☐
Have you done the "Willings" test and the Actions to get
    started?   ☐   ☐
Are you ready to begin your creative process?   ☐   ☐

~~~~~~

Were your answers YES to all these questions? If so, CONGRAT-
ULATIONS! You are clearly committed to bringing out your own
uniqueness. Now you're ready to go on to the next key.

But before proceeding, CELEBRATE—unless you are having
difficulties with any of these areas. If so, go back and re-do the Actions relevant to where you seem stuck.

Keys

   *Acknowledging your own creative potential is vital to becoming a
    fulfilled creator.*

   *Recognition of your uniqueness is key to unlocking your creative
    potential.*

   *Your intention and your willingness to be creative are essential to
    embarking on your creative journey.*

   *Your willingness to spend time alone is an essential key to getting in
    touch with your creative potential.*

   *Do not let your intention to reach your creative goals be sidetracked
    by obstacles, excuses, or critics of any kind.*

~~~~~~~~~~~~~~~~~~~~~~~~~~~~~~~~

Making a Clearing for Your Creative Space

Clearing space for creativity is very important for allowing your creativity to flourish. Spaces in one's life are not just physical, but also mental, emotional, spiritual, and temporal. In clearing all of these, you can then begin making your creative space. The process of investigating and clearing all the other spaces in your life guides you into how to create your own creative space. This chapter will provide guides for beginning to clear the different spaces in your life.

CLEARING ALL THE SPACES IN YOUR LIFE

First of all, what does it mean to clear spaces, and why is it necessary? By "space," we mean a variety of physical and metaphorical environments or conditions. There are five kinds of spaces with which you must be concerned and which you must clear if you are to be creatively productive. These are the five kinds of space:

Mental
Physical
Emotional
Spiritual
Temporal

Clearing all of these lets you open up a special space for creativity—your creative space.

Clearing mental space is when your mind is cleared of worry and other things to do, cleared of all the internal chatter that diverts you from your creative intention.

Clearing physical space means establishing one or several special places where your mind is at its most fertile. For example, this physical space can be a room of your own, a place to dance, or a table in a café.

Clearing emotional space means becoming free, at least for the moment, of emotional obstacles and blocks that might prevent you from fulfilling your creative potential.

Clearing spiritual space means when you allow the spirit—the spirit of God or of the universe, or the sacred spirit within yourself—to flow freely without impediment and be allowed to work within you to bring out your creative potential.

Clearing temporal space occurs when you open up a period of time, free of other activities or distractions, free from other obligations or commitments, and then dedicate that time—however long or short a period—to your creative work.

Only after clearing, for even a brief moment, each of these spaces—mental, physical, emotional, spiritual, temporal—can you then make space for your creative work. For most people, the process has to be repeated over and over, every day, and often throughout the day in order to stay with your creativity.

~ If I am about to begin a major creative project, I often spend several days systematically striving to clear out the other spaces in my life in order to be clear and free to enter a creative space at the set time. In the process, I also try to prepare myself to ward off possible encroachments from various directions into my creative space, in a sense to arm myself with tricks and techniques, mottoes, for preventing mental, physical, emotional, spiritual,

or temporal cluttering that might arise when I'm in my creative space. The more I learn how to do this for large projects, the better I become at practicing these techniques of clearing space on a daily basis for any kind of creative activity. (L.C.)

TAKING STOCK

Now you will be asked to take an inventory of all the spaces in your life and to list those items and areas that are currently preventing your establishing a creative space. Here are guidelines for clearing each of the other spaces in order that you can then establish your own creative space:

Mental Space

In order to clear your mental space, you need to get your daily issues, activities, and chores all out of your head. You must remove other things from your mind, everything that would interfere with openness to your creativity. You need mental clarity.

~ *I had been working on clearing away some depressing thoughts. I once noticed an imaginary black cloud coming my way. It was just big enough to settle above my head. I told it to go away, that I didn't need it. And, much to my surprise, it went away and never came back. I was astonished to find that my direct order for it to go away and leave me alone really worked. I use such directness all the time now whenever any thought comes my way that I do not wish to entertain. My life has been happier and less clouded ever since.* (L.B.)

ACTION 1: Keep a day-timer to list all the activities that come into your mind, whether it is having a meeting, buying Pampers, running errands, or thinking about something that worries you. Once it is on your list, then it is out of your head until the time you have decided you will do or think about it or not.

This helps you organize your life in order to allow you to have creative space for yourself. Then prioritize your list, deciding when to do and think about certain activities. You can also separate your lists into personal and professional. Establish schedules and categories of tasks. This is how you clear your mental space. You can refer back to your day-timer anytime, but for now you will begin to have your mental freedom.

Physical Space

Establish some space that is yours, where you can go for creative work. This could include a variety of kinds of spaces for each particular person, depending on what kind of creative work you plan to do. This could be a space set aside temporarily in which you can work. It might even mean a change of geographical location. If you are a dancer, you probably need a dance studio, but initially you may just use your living room. If you are a writer, you may need a place where you do only your writing, a special room, and also you may want to find another kind of space, like a table at a café or a park bench where you think about your writing. Likewise for any kind of creative work, you need some "sacred space" where you can keep your ideas, your ongoing work, your journals, your notes.

You have to give yourself permission to create your own space, whatever that is, and you must make it off limits to anyone else for their various activities. This is where boundaries come in. This space represents you. It could be simply a desk and a chair in a corner, or a full studio, or a workshop. In this space, you do only your creative work. And you need to make it clear to others that they cannot invade or destroy your special physical space.

ACTION 2: Establish your own particular physical space for your own creative work.

Connecting to Creativity ~

This will be one of the most difficult challenges, to limit your own space and to stick to your resolve even though others will try to invade it and also you yourself will be tempted to use it for other activities. Here, though, you must be firm with both yourself and others that at least this particular physical space is for your particular creative work.

Emotional Space

Emotional space involves all the feelings and passions that come up in your life at any particular time. Many such emotions dominate our lives and prevent us from working creatively. But, at the same time, these very emotions can become the subjects or fabric of your creative production. The aim in clearing your emotional space, therefore, is that rather than allowing your strongest emotions to consume you negatively or destroy and distract you, you will transform them into a creative act and product. It is the creative use of these powerful emotions and passions that turns negative, destructive energy into creatively positive work.

~ Much of my creative writing is about very painful experiences of my life that I am transforming into works of art. One time when I was desperately trying to tell the story of these very painful incidents in my writing, some friends urged me not to do it. But I knew I had to in order to fulfill myself. The problem was how to re-endure the pain. A therapist, who urged me to continue with my plan to write my story, made a very useful suggestion. She said I could re-live and write the painful story in controlled doses— controlling the amounts as if I were conducting an experiment in chemistry. If the memories of the emotions became too painful, I could stop writing for a while, go away from my work and the pain of the remembered emotion, and return only later for another dosage, the duration of which I could control. (L.C.)

ACTION 3: Identify three subjects of great emotional content for you. Write them down. Imagine how you would express these passions creatively.

Would you make a painting? Write a story or poem? Decorate your house? Dance? Or make a meal? These emotions, the great passions of your life, will become the subjects of your best work.

Spiritual Space

In this creative process, you are becoming both a receiver and a transmitter. This is the time when you're opening your heart and soul to the messages that you will then be acting upon—creating. It involves a kind of faith in the process that you will allow the creative to come through you to the world. This is your spiritual side. It can mean many different things to different people. And no one need feel they have to be like anyone else in their appreciation of whatever the spiritual means to them.

In order to clear and then direct your spiritual space, you might try any number of kinds of activities. You can practice meditation or yoga or tai chi. You can pray. You can practice any kind of religion. You can walk on the beach. You can swim in the ocean or a pool. You can seek evidence of our connection to the spirit. You can seek spiritual growth through all kinds of therapy.

What you are doing here in clearing your spiritual space is to tune in to your own internal guidance system. Whatever does it, whatever gets you from the outside to the inside and works for you, that is what you want to do here.

Clearing your spiritual space is a very "alone" activity, and you must ultimately be prepared to work on this alone. Even when you attend a group religious service or work with a therapist or participate in a group meditation, what happens to you in this process, how you clear your spiritual space, depends on you alone and how you receive the spirit in your life.

Connecting to Creativity ~

ACTION 4: Choose an activity that will encourage your spiritual growth in order to prepare yourself for being more productive when you enter your creative space.

In this spiritual space, it is very possible that you may begin to get indications, messages, about how to evoke your creativity. Clearing spiritual space is a critical preparatory ground for entering your creative space. Here in this spiritual space you will begin to acknowledge your role as a conduit for creativity and ideas. Acknowledging the spiritual aspect of your life paves the way for exciting, creative journeys.

Temporal Space

Now that you have cleared your mental and physical spaces, re-directed your emotional space, and tuned in to your spiritual side, you can establish special temporal space to devote to your creative space. How long does it take to be creative? You can't say how long. You can't anticipate the time it will take to create what you want to create. You can't force time. And time is never a measure of success. On the other hand, deadlines can prove very helpful in pushing you to be creative. There are also times, too, when you seem to be getting nowhere, and then you have to let go of a particular effort. What is important is to give yourself enough time to allow the creative juices to flow.

ACTION 5: Establish a set period of time each day or each week in which you will be in your special physical space to be in your creative space.

In the beginning, this could mean only fifteen minutes a day. But as with any exercise, you can slowly begin to build up the length of time you are involved with this creative endeavor—and you will gradually begin to realize what works for you. Just as you set time to go to work, eat meals, run errands, meet friends, you must now clearly set times to be in your creative space. It is very important that during this time you do not allow interruptions and you protect your space for this creative work.

Creative Space

Now that you have cleared, re-worked, opened up, all the five major spaces of your life, you are ready for the very important step of setting up your own creative space. This creative space will be defined by its own physical, mental, emotional, spiritual, and temporal dimensions. Your creative space will evolve at particular times in the beginning, in a particular physical space and within the cleared framework of your unique mental, emotional, and spiritual context. If you acknowledge that your creative space represents part of your own essence, then you will want to honor and protect it just as you would your own person. This creative space will be sacred to you.

ACTION 6: Establish your own creative space.

Ideally, at first, you will devote an hour a day or one day of each week to your creative space. Steadily, over time, you will begin to dedicate more and more of your life to this very special, sacred creative space. It is YOUR creative space.

Keys

  Clearing space for creativity is very important for allowing your creativity to flourish.

  Clearing all the other spaces in your life—mental, physical, spiritual, emotional, and temporal—is not a one-time activity.

  The clearing must take place constantly and will help make you more creative in every aspect of your life.

~~~~~~~~~~~~~~~~~~~~~~~~~~~~~~~~

Paying Attention to Inner and Outer Signals

Start now in your creative space to pay attention to your inner and outer signals. This paying special attention to your inner voices and inner desires, as well as to your perceptions of the world, is a critical step in leading you to your creative expression.

INNER SIGNALS: BEING AWARE OF THE WORLD INSIDE YOU

Mindfulness—hearing and receiving your own inner messages, paying attention to your inner self—is a process that needs to go on all the time, everywhere you are. It is essential to creativity. You will then carry this inner attentiveness into all areas of your life.

~ *People have always called me courageous because I have left good jobs, left a marriage, struck out on my own, followed my star. I have never felt courageous. I now know that what people see as courageous in me is my own instinctual understanding about following my inner voices. I never questioned those voices and always followed them. Sometimes guidance came from the outside, as when a ballet teacher recommended that I go to the Juilliard School, even though at the time, I didn't even know about the place. Somehow I have always instinctively known what direction to go with my art and my creative life. Fortunately, I also had parents who eventually supported me in my choices.* (L.B.)

This section focuses on the inner messages revealed through your night dreams and daydreams. Learning to pay attention to inner thoughts and outer voices you can hear throughout your life, noticing what you like to do and also what you do not like to do, will bring your desires to consciousness.

What are these inner signals and where are they? They are our gut-feelings. They are what is called intuition. They are our immediate likes and dislikes. Listening to all your messages is the beginning of self-knowledge. What you're thinking about, what you're feeling—these insights—are the beginning of the definition of the self, the identifying aspects of your uniqueness.

~ *I was directing a very exciting summer program in the arts for teachers when one evening I ran out of film for the camera I was using to document the program. It was early evening, and I asked my son if he wanted to go to the drugstore with me to buy some film. As we were driving along in the car, suddenly, almost as if the steering wheel was out of my control, I turned down a quiet street following a sign for a housing development. I said to my son, "Want to take a side trip to see something different?" Sure enough, I had stumbled upon our next house, which turned out to be a great buy, a wonderful place to raise a family, and became one of my most exciting home-decorating adventures.* (L.B.)

~ *Throughout my life, when I have heeded my own inner voices (the first, usually simple ones that seem to repeat instructions to me), I have found that these inner instructions were right. These messages have both guided me in the creative directions I have sensed I should move and also required that I be creative in the way I have lived my life. Often these inner instructions were in direct opposition to those more conservative, careful suggestions my parents and friends might offer with all kindness, but without the inner understanding of my own personal and creative needs. Following these inner messages, I have taken huge risks in my life, risks of going far away, changing direction, moving in new directions that have often required constant creativity. Though often very difficult and sometimes painful, I never regretted them in the long run. In retrospect, too, I have always been amazed at how right the messages were for me but often in ways that were not apparent at the time. It was almost as if I had a secret knowledge of the direction I needed to go in spite of the fact that I was certainly not conscious of it. I have always just had strong gut-feelings.* (L.C.)

ACTION 1: Off the top of your head, without deep reflection, list what immediately comes to mind in terms of ideas or inner directions, feelings you have about what you are supposed to do with your life in order to be fulfilled creatively. List all the inner signals that you can think of that come to mind without restricting or editing them. Just write them down here or in your journal.

_____

_____

_____

_____

_____

LIKES AND DISLIKES

Noticing what you like to do and what you do not like to do will bring your desires to consciousness. This is very important for moving in your creative direction. Trying to conform to some idea of who you think you need to be can be very misleading and eventually can disenfranchise you from yourself. Going along with everyone so as not to rock the boat or put anyone in turmoil can make you into a robot-like person with no desires and no authentic personality. Identifying what you like and what you dislike is a good step to discovering your unique being.

ACTION 2: Make a list of the things you like doing and what you do not like doing. Also, list the things you might want to try but have not yet tried. This is the beginning of self-awareness, which is an important ingredient in reaching your creative potential.

Like	*Don't Like*	*Want to Try*
_____	_____	_____
_____	_____	_____
_____	_____	_____
_____	_____	_____
_____	_____	_____
_____	_____	_____

MORNING THOUGHTS AND FEELINGS

In the morning, just upon awakening, you are at your most vulnerable and most open to inner challenges and insights. This is a special time to lie quietly, without discussion, and pay attention to your thoughts and feelings. It is very important not to let yourself be disturbed at this critical time. Letting yourself be alone with your thoughts for at least five to fifteen minutes is suggested. Ideally, you would continue lying in bed until your thoughts are complete. If you have had dreams the night before, try to remember every part of them. (See the section on "Dreams" on page 39.) See if at this time solutions to problems come to you. Open all your channels at this time. If nothing is coming, ask for guidance. This simple request for help can often open up many connections to solving problems in your creative activity. Be as specific as possible in your requests.

ACTION 3: Wake up in the morning and immediately pay attention to what you're thinking about at that first moment. Let your thoughts and feelings just flood through your mind. Try not to cut this flow off. Then, after this initial morning session, write down everything that seems important to remember.

_____

_____

_____

_____

_____

The early morning, or whatever time of day it is that you first wake up, is also believed by many to be the ideal time for doing your most creative work. If you are unaccustomed to taking advantage of this first-waking time for working alone on creative activities, you should at least try it out to see if you find it to work for you.

~ *Whenever I have a critical piece or section to write or a plan to set forth, I plan the night before to get up immediately upon waking and then immediately write the work or outline the plan. I know that at that time I will have my clearest, freshest thoughts on that subject. At such times, I know I must be disciplined not to do anything else first, not to let any other distractions, like the news, enter into my mind until I've written what comes.* (L.C.)

DREAMS

Dreams are some of the most important transmitters of messages in our lives. They are often complex, and they are always symbolic. After dreaming, you may try to figure them out because they are puzzles revealing secrets of our lives. For most people, it is very important to write down the details of their dreams immediately upon awakening from the dream. Occasionally, people can also remember forgotten but important details of dreams some time later after waking. Whenever the information comes from the dream, it is important to write everything down that you can possibly remember. Also, it's important to write down dreams over time, because often they're in a series in which the meaning may not become clear until weeks, months, or even years later.

ACTION 4: Write down all the details you can remember from your dreams immediately upon waking each morning. Start with any you remember from last night.

_____

_____

_____

_____

_____

Also, write down all the interpretations of your dreams you can imagine. After some time—days, months, years—go back and look over all you have written about various dreams. You will probably discover patterns and series of dreams that provide important messages about the directions for your life.

ACTION 5: You may become so interested in your dream-world, its messages and meanings for your life, that you will want to study various theories of dream-interpretation and methods of dream-work. To help you toward fulfilling your creative potential, we suggest you consider reading books on dreams or taking dream-courses.

~ *The role of dreams in guiding my creative life could be another whole book or more. But, suffice it to say, messages from my dreams have been as important as those other intuitive inner voices that I have constantly tried to heed and incorporate into the creative decisions of my life. Sometimes the messages from my dreams come from the dominant images, sometimes from actual words spoken, sometimes from the whole dream or a series of dreams, and I sense, too, that I am unconsciously but constantly influenced by dreams I cannot even remember. Once a dream a whole year beforehand led eventually to my enrolling in an inspiring week-long seminar on dream-work. By paying attention to that dream at the time, then remembering it much later, I was actually guided to a place and community of people that had a major, positive effect on my creative life.* (L.C.)

SYNECTICS

Pay attention to merging ideas and words, images that seem similar even though at first glance they appear to be different and uncon-nected. Throughout the day, continue to pay attention to every-thing that interests you, repulses or attracts you. Listen to all the messages that come to you throughout the day, no matter how ir-relevant they may seem. Much of your creative work will come from connecting ideas, words, images, symbols, that you initially considered disparate. These are the evidence of what we call "syn-ectics" in your own life.

~ *For the first few years out of college, I had been in the field—publish-ing—that I had always thought was where I wanted to be. Yet I had a strong sense of dissatisfaction with it but had no idea what else to do. Then one day a friend happened to mention something about film-editing, and that made me think of how I have always loved movies and imagining how they are made, put together. Then I remembered reading recently about a special course in digital film-editing and recalled how the idea at the moment had attracted me but I'd then quickly put it out of my mind. But there it was again—still there, ready to bounce up at me. Suddenly, my mind went back to my childhood, and I remembered how I loved working in my room, making things, putting things together. Over the next year or so, the idea of film-editing kept coming back to mind more and more frequently, until, finally, I realized that I had to take a great leap of faith in my various inner messages and change fields. Once I made that decision, I felt so happy that I knew it was right, even though I have no idea what the future will hold for me in this field. What's interesting to me, also, is that now I realize my training in publishing and editing, and my undergraduate major in literature, will all prove to be very important foundations for my new film-editing career. Strangely, though, I realize I could not have planned this seemingly necessary sequence of events.* (J.P.)

SYNCHRONICITY

Pay attention to any remarkable events or people or other things coming together, some of which appear to be coincidental but are actually synchronistic. The idea of synchronicity is that things happening at the same time or coming together in your life at once are not necessarily happenstance but may in fact be interpreted as having meaning and significance as signs and patterns in your life. Start noticing when synchronistic patterns begin to occur in your life. These could be guides to the direction of your creative journey. These people and events might be signposts that will help you along your way.

~ It's really strange that I should be meeting you at this moment. For the past few days and weeks, I've been thinking a lot about what to do with my life and how I want to be creative but don't know what to do. And I've been telling myself that I must pay attention to any kind of signs that might show up in even my daily routine. Then, suddenly, we start talking on the plane, and, to my amazement, you tell me about your interest in creativity and how you and your friend are writing a book about how to tap into the creative

process—exactly what I've been trying to figure out how to do. What's really amazing is that I hardly ever strike up conversations with passengers on flights, but for some reason—I thought you looked interesting—I decided to speak to you and ask what you do. Now my mind is jumping with ideas about what to do. I think that's what they call synchronicity—that I'd been thinking about this and then met you. (M.P.)

ACTION 6: Keep jotting notes in your journal throughout the day about anything that occurs in your life and your mind that may provide clues for your creative directions.

In particular, jot down any creative ideas that come to you throughout the day. If you do not note them when they come to you, you'll probably never remember them later. Think back over your life to discover examples of synectics and synchronicity. Describe what happened, the sequence of events, and what unfolded as a result of your becoming aware of such synectistic and synchronistic phenomena in your life.

EPIPHANIES AND EVEN VISIONS

Open yourself up to and allow the possibility of epiphanies—those "aha" moments in your life when, suddenly, you understand or comprehend something or know exactly what to do. You may be one of the fortunate people who have what might be called "visions" or epiphanies, moments of great clarity and understanding that occur in a flash or in a space of time that seems very powerful. Perhaps more people have such experiences than realize it. Unfortunately, in the modern world, many people are afraid to acknowledge that they have been given such incredible moments. Usually such experiences occur when one is in a creative space, and the moments of vision and epiphany can transform you.

~ *I was very fortunate to have had what I call "a vision" that changed, or rather re-oriented the direction, of my creative endeavors for a while. I didn't actually see anything. It was more like a set of instructions that were given to me over a period of about eight hours while, stone sober, I sat bolt upright in my bed and listened without argument, without allowing any of my old inner critics to say "no." The message was that I was to return to my childhood dream of being a journalist—a dream that I had completely abandoned for the ten years since I had graduated from college. The vision occurred when I had taken myself out of my old life, removed myself geographically to a faraway place and had actually embarked on another career path. The vision was so powerful that it stayed in front of my mind for years as I slowly proceeded toward following the detailed instructions of that memorable night. For years afterwards, too, I celebrated the anniversary of that vision every October and the creative changes it had brought to my life.* (L.C.)*

ACTION 7: Take the time to think back over your life, and write down any time in which you have had any kind of vision or epiphany about something you should do in your life, about how to look at your life.

If you think deeply about this, you may well discover that you have had such epiphanies, possibly visions, even though you may not have called them that at the time. They are events that flash momentarily into your life and have a transforming effect about how you look at the world or the direction you should move.

Paying special attention to your inner voices, inner desires, is a critical step in leading you to your creative expression. Hearing and receiving your own inner messages, paying attention to your inner self, is a process that needs to go on all the time, everywhere, throughout all your life. It is essential to your creativity.

OUTER SIGNALS: BEING AWARE
OF THE WORLD AROUND YOU

Paying attention to outer signals from the world around you is equally important. In becoming aware of the outside world you will become more cognizant of and discriminating about what attracts you. Being aware not only of what attracts you now but also expanding your awareness of the beauty all around you helps make you more creative. This is the critical, mindfulness side of creativity.

This section helps you become mindful of the sounds, sights, ideas, language, movements, people, nature, that surround and attract you. These are all signposts about what you're interested in and what will come out in your own creative expression.

ACTION 8: Make a list of all the kinds of outer signals that immediately come to mind as signposts you already know exist in your life.

_____

_____

_____

_____

_____

~ I was so excited by the beauty I found in the outer world that I began to realize that I am visually stimulated by patterns and vistas and movement. Turning to photography to try and capture this beauty, I found that the skills I had developed as a choreographer made me see compositions through the lens of the camera. I began photographing everything that interested me visually and have exhibited my photography in galleries. I am working to find ways to integrate my photographic slides with my dances and my poetry with my photography. (L.B.)

SOUNDS

Your aural sense can be keen if you allow it to be. Notice what sounds annoy you or please you and attract you. Become aware of what you do hear and what you block out. Do you hear the words of the song or just the melody? Which sounds appeal to you that tell you about yourself? Do sounds delight you? Are you at heart a musician? Do you want to make sounds? Do you want to make music?

ACTION 9: Listen to all the sounds you can possibly hear. Close your eyes and try to identify all the sounds you can hear within a three-minute time span. How far can you hear? How close can you hear? Make a list of these sounds.

_____

_____

_____

_____

_____

~ *When I taught in Virginia, I liked to take my students to a beautiful arboretum nearby so that they could experience running and leaping in the meadow, hugging trees, communing with nature, and listening intently to all the sounds they could hear in that place, either near them or far away. It was always an extraordinary day for these students. For one young man, who had grown up in the city and had never been in the country, this was his first excursion into true nature, and it changed his life.* (L.B.)

SIGHTS

Become more aware of everything in your line of vision, every-thing you can see. Notice the whole view as well as the details. Notice the shapes, the landscape, the density. Would you like to paint the landscape you see? Does the sight inspire you to write? Would you like to dance in the meadow that you see? Do you want to make a song about what you see? Do you want to write a poem about what you behold? Does the sight in front of you turn you on to wanting to express your vision in any of these ways?

Do you delight in color, texture, shapes, and patterns?

~ *Everywhere I go, anytime, I am always aware of texture and color and lines and light. I keep notes about my observations and make sketches wherever I am. Then, I refer to these, and, of course, they are in my subconscious, whenever I am painting.* (A.W.)

ACTION 10: Observe the way you respond to all the sights you see in a five-minute time span. Write down which colors, shapes, and settings most attract you.

_____

_____

_____

_____

_____

LANGUAGE

Become aware of the language spoken and written around you. That includes the different languages spoken as well as the accents and the use of language. Pay attention to the words, the inflections, the accents, the structure of the variety of language you encounter all the time. Become very conscious of all the ways language and languages are used. Do words and sentence-structure delight you?

Do you love to read? Do you want to write? Are you drawn to play with words and languages? Do you want to make beauty with language?

ACTION 11: Note, write down, those words and phrases that especially catch your attention over a day. Write down the books you hear about and want to read.

_____

_____

_____

_____

_____

THE WHOLE WORLD AROUND YOU

Being aware, becoming mindful, of everything around you contributes much to your being able to bring out the most creative gifts you have. You can now do these same kinds of Actions, ask the same kinds of questions as above, for all the other wonderful things around you. What colors attract you? What movements attract you? What in nature attracts you? What in people and what about people attract you? What smells attract you? What kinds of touch attract you?

ACTION 12: Begin recording in your journal all your observations about these other elements in the world around you.

Everything you are mindful of is a clue to your own self-expression. You, as a creative person, will all the time be aware of and appreciate beauty around you. You are now looking at the world with the eyes of an artist. Artists are connoisseurs of beauty and their environment.

Connecting to Creativity ~

Keys

- Paying attention to your own inner signals and to outer signals from the world around you is very important.

- In becoming aware of the outside world, you will become more cognizant of and discriminating about what attracts you.

- Being aware not only of what attracts you but also of the beauty all around you helps make you more creative.

- Being aware of the world around you is the critical, mindfulness side of creativity and contributes greatly to the fulfillment of your creative process.

KEY 4

~~~~~~~~~~~~~~~~~~~~~~~~~~~~~~~

Staring into Space and Doing Nothing

Mindlessness. Staring into space and doing nothing—strange as it may seem—are among the most critical aspects of creativity. Yet they are perhaps the least understood components of the creative process. This means that you take time in your daily life to stop and do nothing—"to smell the roses."

This chapter introduces you to the okay-ness of "mindlessness"—to the idea that what in Western culture is called "wasting time" is critical to the creative process. Giving yourself permission to spend time doing nothing and just staring into space is a critical activity in the growth and development of creative ideas.

ACTION 1: Think of times in your life, during your day, when you already allow yourself to practice mindlessness. Write down and describe these times. Where are you when you are practicing mindlessness? What are the conditions that allow you to engage in mindlessness? How do you feel at such times of mindlessness?

_____

_____

_____

_____

_____

Much of contemporary society pushes people to be active all the time. Unfortunately, for some people, it even takes getting sick before they stop and "do nothing." Then they find that all kinds of new ideas suddenly start coming to them.

~ Over my life, whenever I have been sidelined in bed, after a surgical operation, the muse always returns instantly to me, and I write lots of poetry. (M.W.)

To enter this mindless state, this "doing nothing," does not require any particular techniques. Mindlessness just requires that you allow yourself truly to let your mind go, to be free, to sit or stand and "do nothing." The effect can be similar to the states reached in meditation, and, perhaps, it can be argued that it is a form of meditation, but it seems important to realize that this state of mindless doing nothing is different. Both can be practiced anywhere, anytime, but the mindlessness is really just that—doing nothing, thinking of nothing, for moments of time throughout your day and life.

SOLITUDE

What this is really about is your being alone. Basically, this non-activity requires you to be bold in determining the exact nature of your own solitude. Solitude is a state of mind, a state of being. It is being alone even when you are in a crowd. It is being able to tune out completely and to go into your own solitude at the same time that you are in a crowd or surrounded by people.

~ As a woman—and many men, too, feel this way—I used to feel shy about going to places alone and sitting by myself. Other people certainly do stare at loners as if they are failures for having to be alone. (Actually, they

should be admiring and envious that the person sitting alone has that free-
dom.) In restaurants, for example, the maitre d's and waiters often ask in a
somewhat condescending way, "Only one?" or "Just alone?" Over the past
few years, however, I've overcome my shyness and just boldly sit alone in
many places as I've realized more and more how much I need to be alone at
times throughout the day in order to re-align myself, to re-focus on my cre-
ative projects. (L.C.)

It is critical that you give yourself permission to stare into space
and do nothing. It is critical that you give yourself permission to
enjoy solitude on a regular basis. If you wish to live up to your creative potential, you cannot miss discovering solitude. It is the great
treasure of a creative person's life. You need to find places in which
you can do nothing, in which you are in solitude and can practice
mindlessness. You must ask those closest to you to honor your need
for time alone.

~ *It took years for me to make a singular act. I thought about many things*
I wanted to do by myself, but I was too afraid to act on my ideas. But now I
love to be alone. It gives me time to think, to be aware of my feelings. Yet
sometimes I find that it is still difficult for me to be alone for long if I am
doing nothing. I really have to fight my temptation to call somebody or go
somewhere with someone, instead of going alone. At such times, the old feel-
ings return—that somehow I feel I am protected if someone is with me, pro-
tected from feeling my discomfort, even protected from myself. After all,
when I am alone, my mind is free to think of many things, and most often I
think about my life, my desires, my hopes, and my dreams. (L.B.)

Connecting to Creativity ~

ACTION 2: Take an inventory of what activities allow you to be in solitude.
When can you be in solitude and where? Here, or in your journal, describe in
detail these experiences of solitude.

_____

_____

_____

_____

_____

APPEARING TO BE DOING NOTHING

To understand the power of this necessary time of quiet growth—
of appearing to be doing nothing—in our creative process, we
need only look at nature as an example of the need for a gestation
period. The bulbs that we plant in the fall need the time under the
earth throughout the winter in order to bloom in the spring. And,
of course, the baby in the womb has to grow in hiding for nine
months before coming into the world. To the naked eye, it may at
first appear as if nothing is happening in these cases. But for all living creatures, these periods of gestation are vital. In all cases we
have to trust in the process that something is happening.

_~ People have often teased me about how I can take naps almost anywhere
and do so every day. Naps, in fact, have been the salvation of my life and
have allowed me to live a very creative life, first as a mother and home-maker
and later as a legislator and political activist. My days are always so full of
people and activities, but I have always made time—at least fifteen minutes
a day—to do nothing by taking naps, wherever I can—alone in a room or,
if that's not possible, sometimes just off in a corner with people milling all
around or in a car with someone else driving._ (M.W.)

~ *I always take the summers off from teaching—to regenerate myself. I somehow am able to give myself permission "to do nothing" during these times. If I don't allow myself this time of doing nothing, I know that I will not be my best and most creative self again when the new year rolls around.* (L.B.)

~ *I find that to be creative in all aspects of my life, I need to drop out and do nothing on a fairly regular basis. The best way for me to do nothing is to go fishing—just stand there with nothing on my mind and idly pull in and throw back the line from time to time. Usually I go fishing on weekends but I also try to go on my lunch break as often as possible since I work near the water. When I return from an hour of fishing, I find my mind is clear of junk and full of creative new ideas for my next projects.* (J.C.)

~ *As a child and even as a young person in college and later as a teacher in Africa, I let myself go into states of "mindlessness," without even consciously realizing how critical this was for the creative process. But when I entered what is known as the "rat-race," the regular, fast-paced jobs and life that most of us think we have to have to survive, then it was extremely difficult ever to take times out to be "mindless." That world frowns on people who appear to be doing nothing at any point in their day. It was many years before I felt confident enough again about my own beliefs in what I need for being creative that I began to give myself hours and days of "doing nothing," literally staring out windows, mindlessly watching crowds, observing birds, squirrels, and cats. Now I have to let myself go regularly into these trance-like states of mindlessness.* (L.C.)

~ *Sitting by a swimming pool and staring into space for a little while each day give me the kind of creative energy I need to dream up the kinds of business deals I have to throughout my day. Often I take a dip as well, but it's the sitting and staring that really clear my mind to do my best work the rest of the day in a high-pressured world.* (T.C.)

What does it mean to do nothing? Exactly what it says—do nothing. Here are some suggestions of do's and don'ts:

Do	Don't
Wander aimlessly.	Have a special purpose.
Stare out the window.	Clean the windows.
Swim, walk, run, dance alone.	Compete.
Drive a long distance in your car.	Listen to audio tapes.
Waste time.	Stick to a schedule.
Watch your cats, the ants, birds.	Watch television.
Take a nap.	Keep the radio on.
Take a long bath.	Read a magazine.
Sit and stare at nowhere.	Look at your watch.

You can add to these lists.

_____

_____

_____

_____

_____

PERIODS OF GERMINATION

In the case of your own creative development, you must constantly allow yourself these periods of gestation, when to the outside world you probably appear to be doing nothing. Staring into space and doing nothing are activities you, as a creative person, will need to engage in daily, weekly, always—before, during, and after all your creative work.

~ Key 4 Staring into Space and Doing Nothing

This is a period of dormancy within the creative process. This is the critical time when many ideas come to you, or perhaps no ideas come at all for a while.

~ *The hardest thing for me to do is "do nothing"—to wander, to day-dream, to be unaccountable. As much as I love to do it, I feel guilty. I make excuses for what I did all day. I find that other people do the same thing. Instead of acknowledging something that we all need and all secretly do, we make up stories as to what we hope people will think that we did. Yet this much needed time of germination is so unacknowledged that people get sick to get it, zone out in front of the television to get it, and sometimes become street people to get enough "time out."* (L.B.)

In giving yourself periods of germination, times when you appear to be doing nothing, you must wait patiently for ideas, for insights, for critical creative connections, for desires to be expressive in specific ways. This time—of staring into space and doing nothing—is the most valuable time you can spend in preparation for your creative work. It is also the time when you need the most faith in the process because nothing may happen, and maybe it won't for a very long while. But then, again, maybe it will. Please do not give up this non-activity just because you do not get tangible results right away. Just trust that this is something you have to do.

~ *Whenever I have had major creative projects, I have given myself weeks, sometimes months, to wander around, appearing to everyone else to be doing nothing. Instead, I know that I am then in a great period of germination, and I just have to relax and let it all unfold. I remember the summer I had a major book contract, and a friend of mine had been worried that I would not write it because she realized I was "doing nothing." When I finally set the day to begin the work, which by then was fully formed in my head after the weeks of germination, my friend stopped by to bring me food and was amazed at the organization of my work and what I had accomplished before-hand by "doing nothing." Then, after the germination, the book just rolled out of my head.* (L.C.)

ACTION 3: List at least three times during the past week when you stared into space and did nothing, absolutely nothing, for at least ten minutes. Describe what happened, where you were at the time, and whether you came up with any insights.

_____

_____

_____

_____

_____

COURAGE

All of this requires tremendous courage of your conviction about yourself and your own creativity because engaging in this non-activity of staring into space and doing nothing will bring the most criticism from friends, family, and colleagues. Most people do not understand this. Be prepared for criticism from people who do not understand the value of doing nothing.

It takes a lot of courage to take this step into nothingness, into uncharted territory. Here is where a leap of faith into the unknown is required and your trust in the process and in your passion is tested. While there are no guarantees, we believe that if you have faith in pursuing your creative potential and explore what comes from doing nothing, then things will emerge for you in this creative encounter.

~ As a woman in conventional society, I have never been encouraged to be alone. Something has always been foreboding about it, something wrong about being alone. Is it about my independence? The decision to be alone and attempt to fulfill one's creative potential has a kind of defiance about it—a striking out on one's own, to find one's own way, to be a freethinker, deciding things for oneself. It is an independent act—the power of self-ness. (L.B.)

ACTION 4: List who in your life you think will be critical of your need for solitude, for times to be alone and do nothing. Who in your life will criticize you if you spend several hours doing nothing, producing nothing? What do you think they will say? Include your own internal critics and be prepared to deal with them.

_____

_____

_____

_____

_____

PREPARING FOR CRITICISM

This is a crucial time for you to plan and make decisions about how you will react, or, better yet, not react, to someone who criticizes you for not doing anything when they expected you to produce something tangible during your solitude. You must be prepared to respond, or not respond, when they say, "What! You haven't accomplished anything in the past few hours of sitting around. What were you doing?" Realize that often what appears to be criticism may just be small talk because those people don't know what to say to you. On the other hand, you will have to be prepared to receive actual criticism. In such cases, you need to prepare yourself to respond as minimally and non-defensively as possible. Here's where you need the courage of your conviction that doing nothing can be a positive activity.

ACTION 5: List five responses you can make to criticism about your apparent "wasting time."

1. _____

2. _____

3. _____

4. _____

5. _____

Do not forget that all of this leads to your contributing your unique gifts. Do not give up now. Do not forget that part of your life's path is to find your unique expression and that you must go through this process in order to get there.

~ Not until I was able to discard the things and people that did not belong in my life did I begin truly to find out who I was and to begin to love myself. Even though I built a new life, I found myself again needing to strip away the people and the things that I kept adding into my life, until again I was taken down to my bare bones of existence, to my essence. When will I finally understand that this is, on the whole, a solitary journey and that just as I feel the need to garnish myself with more, the universe pushes me to go it alone—to simplify, to pare down. (L.B.)

One thing is certain—the more you become used to practicing solitude, the more you will like it and never wish to give it up. The treasures you will find in solitude you will never find anywhere else. Again, too, this is all part of the "selfing" process and not a selfish act. The more you grow into your unique being, the more your loved ones will begin to appreciate the unique and wonderful human being you are becoming.

Does it matter to you enough to continue with this process?

Are you committed to fulfilling your unique expression—to giving your unique gifts to the world?

Do not give up now as this gets tougher. Your pay-off is not far away.

You might also now begin to think to yourself: "Nothing is more important than expressing who I really am!"

Remember to repeat your affirmation—especially if and when you begin to doubt your commitment to this process.

> I am unique, and
> > No one else can think what I think
> > Dream what I dream
> > Sing what I sing
> > Say what I say
> > Create what I create.

Key

Staring into space and doing nothing are vital to creativity.

~~~~~~~~~~~~~~~~~~~~~~~~~~~~~~~~~~

Finding Your Creative Direction

In a sense, you are now past the hardest part. You have done the preparation—opened yourself to the creative process. Here the fun begins. It is time to sort through all the different messages and find the right direction for you at this time in your life. Now tune in to your unique and very special self. This chapter will help you decide what form of expression best suits you now.

CHOOSING YOUR FORM OF EXPRESSION

How do you know what's the right direction for you? How do you sort out all the messages that come to you about what form of expression best suits you at this time in your life? What are your passions? What is your innate talent? How do you want to express yourself? In what form do you wish to project your creativity? It is time to choose.

You have acknowledged to yourself that you have something creative you wish to express. You have cleared your spaces. You have listened to your inner signals. You have become aware of the outer messages in the world around you. You have allowed yourself the time to sit and stare and do nothing, to let yourself be open to your creative potential. Now you are ready to choose the way in which you wish to express your creativity.

Instinctively, a person knows what form she or he wants to use for self-expression, but this may not be clear immediately, and, in fact, you may initially sense the desire to try another form. All forms and media of expression are different and can fulfill different needs. This is not an intellectual decision, not something you can justify or even explain logically. This is an instinctual decision.

It is an intuitive choosing. You will feel it in your gut. You will feel your whole body resonate and get excited when you come close to your choice. It is like tuning in to a radio station. First, there is static before you find the crystal clear wavelength of the station. Tune in to your own particular wavelength.

~ *While I often have visions in mind and observations waiting to get out, I don't always know how I should put them out—whether into words, or pictures, or songs.* (P.P.)

This chapter is about how to sort all the messages, inner and outer, and then select your form and medium of expression. It is enough to say simply, "I want to do this, to express myself creatively in this particular way." To help you get started, we have designed a series of quizzes with questions that we believe will help you choose your form of expression. Each test is followed by an Action that we hope will surprise you into discovering unexpected interests. Do the Actions in order, and we suggest you do not look ahead because the importance here is to elicit your most spontaneous responses to the question in order to shock you into acknowledging—and possibly even discovering for the first time—what you truly want to be doing at this time in your life.

This is now the critical time to look into yourself and decide what form of creative expression will work best for you. This is a very exciting time. Let your feelings be free. You want to be open, to be very conscious of all that attracts you.

Connecting to Creativity ~

ACTION 1: First of all, before you take the first test, off the top of your head, write down here or in your journal the forms of creative expression that most attract you—the fields in which you would like now to do your creative work. Do not take time to reflect. Just write your first ideas. At this point, we are not giving you a list of options because we want you to write only what comes to your mind immediately.

_____

_____

_____

_____

_____

CREATIVE ACTIVITIES

Take time out from your life to explore different forms of expression. Have you ever wanted to sing? To dance? To write a poem? To invent something? To come up with a new way of doing business? To create a new product? To re-decorate your house?

Let your imagination go wild.
Envision yourself doing all kinds of creative activities.
Go to science and technology museums, and imagine you are an inventor.
Go to art galleries, and imagine you are one of the artists.
Go to concerts, and imagine you are one of the musicians or one of the dancers.
Spend time in libraries. Read through books about writers, entrepreneurs, artists.
Go to a movie. Imagine yourself as the writer, the director, the actor, the cinematographer, or even one of the characters in the story.

Go to factories and watch how products are made. Imagine
   inventing the machines.
Go watch a house being built or restored, and imagine
   yourself as the architect or builder.

Do not limit yourself. It's like going on a shopping spree. Take a
broad sweep.

Open yourself to all possibilities. Can you imagine yourself being a singer, a dancer, a poet, a writer, an entrepreneur, a creative
software designer? Make this fun.

Fantasize about this wonderful, creative person that you are.
Enjoy yourself.

ACTION 2: Choose and explore at least five different activities to begin opening yourself up to the many forms of creative expression that might appeal to
you. Go to concerts, art galleries, movies, museums, libraries. Observe, study,
explore, fantasize. After each activity, take time to think about the experience
and all your reactions. Keep a list of and notes about all you do in this exploration.
Record all your observations in your journal.

_____

_____

_____

_____

_____

CREATIVE PREFERENCES

Different modes of expression require different personal and physical preferences and characteristics. Here you will begin to take a
comprehensive inventory of all your creative preferences.

What is your preference—to hear or to see or both? To feel or to think? To reason or to intuit? To move or to sit still? To communicate verbally or non-verbally? To be in large spaces? To be in confined spaces? Are you fascinated with colors, sounds, space, textures, words, design, language, human behavior, stories, emotions? Are you fascinated with patterns, puzzles, organization, structures? What are you drawn to, and what are you passionate about? What are all your passions?

The following quizzes will help you answer all the above questions.

Tendencies

ACTION 3: Choose from the following list those tendencies which best describe you:

I prefer to:

☐ Hear
☐ See
☐ Feel
☐ Think
☐ Reason
☐ Intuit
☐ Move
☐ Be still
☐ Communicate verbally
☐ Communicate non-verbally

Acknowledging your preferred tendencies will help you learn more about who you are and your likely choices for your means of expression. It is important to ask yourself such questions as a means of self-examination to prepare for choosing the particular form of expression that best suits you at this time in your life.

Keep these preferred tendencies in mind as you begin to make your choices in the following Actions.

Fascinations

ACTION 4: Choose all the following with which you are most fascinated:

☐ Colors	☐ Sounds	☐ Space
☐ Movement	☐ Textures	☐ Words
☐ Design	☐ Language	☐ Behavior
☐ Emotions	☐ Puzzles	☐ Patterns
☐ Games	☐ Structure	☐ Ideas
☐ Rhythm	☐ Symbols	☐ Rituals
☐ Order	☐ Melody	☐ Buildings
☐ Chemistry	☐ Tactile	☐ Stories
☐ Physical	☐ Text	☐ Other

Inclinations

Now it is also important to determine your inclinations. You need to think about what best suits your personality in order ultimately to choose the form of expression that best suits you.

ACTION 5: Consider the following inclinations that most suit you and choose the following, noting why each selection appeals to you:

☐ Organization _____
☐ Schedules _____
☐ Deadlines _____
☐ Timelessness _____
☐ Spontaneity _____
☐ Production _____
☐ Solitude _____

☐ Symbolism _____
☐ Collaboration _____
☐ Other _____

Passions

Now is the time to look into yourself and acknowledge what your real passions in life are. What is it that you are really passionate about? What are the activities, the ideas, the people, that are your passions?

The list is endless, but the following are some things that you might be passionate about: cooking, dancing, writing, traveling, decorating, designing, building, singing, sharing, volunteering, teaching, sports, games, animals, quilts, fashion, flowers, birds, sculpture, gardens, movies, theatre, the Internet, the ocean, the mountains, architecture—anything in the world. What are YOUR passions?

ACTION 6: List and ponder all the passions in your life. Also, here or in your journal, you may want to write something about why each is a passion for you.

_____
_____
_____
_____
_____

Remembering Your Childhood Passions

If you are having trouble knowing what you are really passionate about, try to remember what you were passionate about as a child. These early passions, the childhood creative pursuits that made you happy—from finger-painting to fort-construction to designing doll clothes—all usually prove to be good indicators of what you will be passionate about through your whole life. This is probably what you are intended to do, but often you get sidetracked from what it was that you originally intended to do with your life. These early desires—everything you loved doing and what you thought you wanted to do when you grew up—all these are usually signs of what you were meant to fulfill in your life. Think back and pay attention to these early passions, these first signals of what you wanted to do creatively.

*~ All I wanted at five was a box of 48 crayons. I loved the Brilliant Rose and the Silver crayons most of all. My beloved grandfather, thinking there was no difference, got me two boxes of 24s. I tried to hide my disappointment. (*K.P.*)*

*~ When I was a child, I danced everything. I didn't walk through the house. I danced. That is what I thought everybody did. What a shock it was for me when I discovered that I was so different, and that was not how everyone moved through their day. I never stopped dancing. (*L.B.*)*

ACTION 7: List and ponder all the passions of your early childhood—all the things you loved doing and thought you wanted to do when you grew up. Write about all that you can remember about why you loved these particular activities.

_____

_____

_____

_____

_____

~ In many of the courses I teach, regardless of the particular subject, I often begin by having my students talk about their passions. It is a great way to

Connecting to Creativity ~

*have people begin to open up and get to know each other, but, more impor-
tantly, it often gets people thinking about what is most important to them.
What we always find especially interesting is that most people's passions can
be traced back in some way to their childhood interests and loves. The people
who are the happiest with what they are doing as adults are those who say
they are doing something related to what they loved to do or wanted to do
when they were children. (L.C.)*

Recognizing these lifelong passions, loves of your life, and pursuing them—following your childhood dreams—is critical to living a fulfilled life, to reaching your creative potential. Remember
your passions and pursue them. Most likely, they are the forms of
expression for your creative potential.

Personal Preferences

ACTION 8: List all your tendencies, fascinations, inclinations, and passions
that you have selected as attracting you the most.

Tendencies	Fascinations	Inclinations	Passions
_____	_____	_____	_____
_____	_____	_____	_____
_____	_____	_____	_____
_____	_____	_____	_____
_____	_____	_____	_____
_____	_____	_____	_____

All these preferences define who you are and shape the unique
person who is you. You are your choices. You are your preferences.

SELECTING YOUR FORM OF EXPRESSION

Now that you have discovered your personal preferences—your individual tendencies, the qualities that most fascinate you, your particular inclinations and passions—you are getting a clearer idea of what form of expression might best suit you at this time. Now you must refine your selection of a form of expression that seems ideally suited to your expressive needs at this time.

Some possibilities are the following creative roles—circle your choice(s):

playwright, poet, artist, entrepreneur, software designer, dancer, writer, teacher, choreographer, costume-designer, architect, exhibit designer, singer, composer, musician, film-maker, painter, sculptor, print-maker, engraver, potter, songwriter, editor, publisher, traveler, diplomat, film-writer, landscape architect, inventor, scientist, mathematician, computer graphics designer, producer, actor, director, cinematographer, set-designer, muralist, graphic designer, creative advertiser, urban planner, engineer, transportation designer, gardener, home decorator, interior designer, fashion designer, cabinetmaker, jewelry maker, tattoo-maker, and many others . . .

ACTION 9: Now that you have investigated more thoroughly all your creative preferences, write down the forms of creative expression that most attract you. (Please do not worry if this is a different choice from what you wrote in Action I of this key.)

_____

_____

_____

_____

_____

~ *For years, I took orders from my boss, devoted all my energy to his business. I was afraid to offer suggestions, even though I knew it would make the business better. One day I had the best idea of all. Then I knew. It was time to go on my own and devote my ideas to building my own business. My creativity was unleashed.* (K.H.)

~ *I have met many closet dancers. People, particularly women, who always wanted to be dancers, stopped dancing at some point for cultural reasons or because they thought they were too big or because they didn't think they had enough talent. It is not about talent. It is about desire. It is about the experience. It is about the dream. We've let the idea be perpetuated that only the talented can do art-making, can be creative. That is just not true. That idea is dulling our lives.* (L.B.)

ACTION 10: Next, look back over your list of tendencies, fascinations, inclinations, and passions to see whether any or all of these fit the characteristics you think are required for your selected forms of expression. If not, then perhaps you should re-think your choices. You may be drawn to a number of forms of expression, but, for purposes of this initial exercise, we suggest you choose only one.

ACTION 11: Now, after checking above, explain why you have chosen this particular form. If what you have written in Action 10 is different from what you wrote in either Action 1 or 9, consider this discrepancy, and then make a decision as to your preference at this time. Write here or in your journal why you have made this choice as the form of creative expression that best suits you now.

CONGRATULATIONS!

Now you have chosen your form of expression. You may have discovered that you would actually prefer to work in several different fields. If it turns out, however, that you have now chosen a particular form of expression different from what you have always thought was your talent, go ahead and choose this new direction for now—and try it. Do not abandon the form through which you have already been expressing yourself. Just try a new way. It just might be a better path for you.

~ *I have worked in many fields, including a variety of arts, but now I feel I can be most creative pursuing an academic career in which I can re-examine old ideas and come up with new theories about the way society works. Sometimes people from my past say, "Oh, you really should be doing your art," but they don't understand how what I'm doing now—using my creative abilities for my social research—is as satisfying for me at the moment as creating works of art were in the past. And, of course, I may return someday to my artistic endeavors. For now, though, being creative in my academic work is the most satisfying and exciting thing I could be doing.* (M.C.)

~ *For years I had wanted to become an engineer and use my love of mathematics to design structures, and, finally, by working with house-building companies, I managed to save enough to return to get my degree. The problem was I still needed to earn extra money while I was back in school, but I couldn't take on a regular, full-time job. Also, by then, after a lot of work on myself and realizing I wanted to live a more creative life, I wanted all my work to be creatively satisfying. I couldn't figure out what I could do to earn money that would allow me to stay in school and, at the same time, feel personally satisfied with my work. One day I was out driving around and went down the "wrong" road. It was a cul-de-sac, and I had to turn around. As I came to a stop at the end of the road, suddenly, I was aware of the unusual house in front of me and, especially, its unique and beautiful door.*

*Instantly, it hit me——I wanted to design and build doors for houses. Imme-
diately, I started my own door-business, which has been very successful and
has kept me creatively happy while, also, giving me flexibility of schedule
and the income to finish my schooling. It's also given me new ideas for the
direction I might decide to go after I finally finish my degree. (J.M.)*

PREPARING YOURSELF FOR YOUR
FIELD OF CREATIVE EXPRESSION

If you have chosen a field that is new for you or in which you have
little or no training, begin now to learn the skills you will need.
Enroll in courses. Read books about the field. Talk with profes-
sionals. Begin to train yourself. Write down all that you must do
to become skilled in this new field. You may have to spend years
preparing and training for this field. Just remember that it is important now to create an affirming vision in your mind to get you
to that far-off goal. It is never too late to follow your dream and
learn new skills. Do not let the fact that you do not have the skills
to do something that you really want to do prevent you from learning and preparing yourself to be creative in a new field.

ACTION 13: Write here and/or in your journal about all that you will have to
do to prepare yourself for the field you have chosen if it is new to you. Make detailed lists and plans about how you will go about learning the necessary skills and
preparing yourself.

_____

_____

_____

_____

_____

AGAIN, CONGRATULATIONS TO YOU!

What you have just done is to decide on HOW you wish now to express yourself. You are ready to move on to deciding WHAT you want to express. At this critical time, it is important to remind you that you will need endurance, self-discipline, and a good energy level to ride through the difficulties and frustrations that you may encounter as you proceed toward achieving your goals of creative expression.

This is a very exciting moment, and you are now inspired to move forward.

Remember that you are the only one who can share your unique gifts with the world. Only you can manifest what is uniquely creative in yourself.

> I am unique, and
>> No one else can think what I think
>> Dream what I dream
>> Sing what I sing
>> Say what I say
>> Create what I create.

Key

∞ *Instinctively, you know what form (or forms) you wish to use for your creative expression.*

~~~~~~~~~~~~~~~~~~~~~~~~~~~~~~~~~~

Imagining the Creative Act

After all your preparation, this is now the big moment of your creative vision. Here, in your creative space, you will begin to form in your mind's eye what you've been wanting to express.

ENVISIONING

This chapter will guide you into imagined action. It will help you find your own way toward the act of creation, toward forming your own vision. This chapter will suggest how to receive visions and ideas, how to open up to whatever comes, no matter how strange and unusual or seemingly impractical any of it may seem.

Here in "Imagining the Creative Act," you will be concentrating on seeing through the eye of the mind. This is the time of great dreaming and vivid imaginings. Exploring the unknown and taking risks will unlock the door of creative action.

You are beginning to create what appears to be something out of nothing. It was not there before. Only you can create it. It is your thoughts, your visions, your ideas, now about to be brought into reality. You are giving a kind of birth to new ideas and new visions that have never appeared before exactly as you will now form them.

SETTING THE SCENE

You are now going to set the very specific scene for allowing your ideas for the particular work to begin to come together into a form. The French term *mise-en-scène* describes this next step. It includes setting the stage for an act, all the surroundings, the environment specific to one play.

Setting the scene again involves generally clearing all your spaces in order to get into your creative space for this particular project. But it also includes getting your actual physical space of work fully ready for this particular project. It may involve going to another place, perhaps geographically far from your customary location. If so, there you will also want to set the scene and establish the place as your creative space.

This "setting the scene" (*mis-en-scène*) for your creative endeavor is one of the most important events in the entire creative process.

ACTION I: Set the scene for putting your ideas into form, as you have before in preliminary steps.

Step 1: Set aside at least an hour during which you will focus exclusively on forming your ideas.

Step 2: Choose a place where you will be undisturbed by telephones and people, where you can be completely undistracted, in a safe location that is conducive to total solitude, ideally an isolated place—a room in your house, a grove in the woods, some hideaway.

Step 3: Before you actually begin to focus on forming the ideas for your project, prepare the place completely to have it ready for this sole immediate task once you do begin.

Step 4: Perform some sort of initial ritual—like saying the mantra about your uniqueness or burning incense or playing music—that helps form your ideas.

Step 5: Lie down or sit down in a comfortable position in which you have a feeling of complete safety and security.

Step 6: Take five to ten deep breaths that will help center you and oxygenate your body to prepare you for this step of your great work.

DAYDREAMING

Let yourself daydream. This is a different kind of daydreaming. You must allow yourself to dream anything and everything about your coming creative work. You will then notice what seems to jump out at you, what grabs your attention. Pay attention to these messages. Let your thoughts wander.

~ Once I have put myself into a creative space—cleared all the other spaces of my life as much as possible—I then like to lie down, sometimes for hours, staying mostly awake in a semi-conscious state, then let my mind go free and fantasize about whatever comes to mind. At such times of unfettered daydreaming, I often come up with very good ideas about what I want to do with my work. Or, sometimes, the fantasizing process has the effect of clearing my mind even more so that, afterwards, once I get up, the right idea jumps into my mind. (L.C.)

ACTION 2: Begin by just letting yourself daydream. Be open to whatever comes to your mind. Watch your daydreams and thoughts to see what special ideas grab you. You are beginning the process to limit and define the structure and ideas of your creation. Whatever you want to call it—daydreaming, fantasizing, imagining, letting your mind go wild—this step, which often requires repeating, is essential to deciding your idea.

~ When the University of Michigan decided for one semester to have most of their classes concentrate on the Medieval Period, I was given the opportu-

nity to choreograph the marvelous Carmina Burana, *a one-hour piece of music consisting of voice, orchestra, and chorus. It is a popular work for dance as it consists of 26 separate poems set to wonderful, dynamic music by Carl Orff. It had always been one of my favorites and had long been one of my dream pieces to choreograph. At that time in my life, however, it was quite daunting for me since I had never choreographed a dance that long, and I was a bit overwhelmed. As I had the summer to prepare for the intense rehearsals that were before me in the coming fall semester, one hot, lazy afternoon I decided to lie down and listen to the whole piece. As I did, I began daydreaming, imagining the dance taking place in my mind. The dance played out in my head, and I saw the whole dance in my mind's eye. I saw how many people were in each section and exactly what they were doing. It was like being at a dance concert. In my fantasy, I also saw that at the end of the dance, the entire audience rose up out of their seats, applauding the production. As my daydream ended, I got up, alone in my living room, and took a bow to an imaginary cheering audience. And when the music stopped, I immediately wrote down all that I had seen in my daydream, and that was exactly how, months later, the real dance unfolded, including the audience's rising in a cheering, standing ovation. That was one of the most outstanding and phenomenal experiences of my life.* (L.B.)

FOCUSING

You have probably had a lot of ideas already circling around in your head. But now is the time to begin focusing on what you really want to write about, dance about, compose, decorate, change in your business. You are no longer dreaming that you want to create. You are now deciding what you want to create. This requires focusing.

You will now begin to find the theme or focus of what you will eventually create. This means that you outline and limit what you are going to make one dance about, what kind of business you are going to focus on, what you are going to teach about, what you will paint on your canvas, what you are going to write about, what the subject is, what the broad action of your focus will be. It is imperative that you make this selection, that you limit your focus. You are setting the parameters of this project.

ACTION 3: Out of all the ideas that you've been having, select a focus, or a particular direction—a particular set of ideas upon which to focus and begin planning. This is like choosing the subject or a topic for a work. What is your subject? What is the broad area for your focus? Here you are performing a kind of guided-imagery during which you will concentrate on your topic until you settle on the specific focus for your work.

_____

_____

_____

_____

_____

If you get to your subject—the limited focus of your work—right away in this first session, then proceed to Action 4 within the same session. If it takes you the full hour or another similar session of solitude to determine the focus of your work, then wait to do Action 4 until you have reached that point of decision. Write down the ideas that come to you during and after each session.

_____

_____

_____

_____

_____

DETAILING

This is the time for coming up with the details of your project. Let everything come to your mind on this topic, this subject, this focus. At the same time, whenever appropriate, you should write, jot notes, sketch, make any kind of sign, to remind yourself of all these ideas, but do not stop your imagining as you take notes. (In chapter 7, you will learn more about this important step of taking notes and planning your work.)

No matter what you do at this point, do not edit yourself, limit your ideas, cut off your thinking.

ACTION 4: Now that you have chosen a particular focus for expressing your ideas, imagine every detail you can about this topic. Let your mind run wild while focused on this one subject. Here, again, you are performing a kind of guided-imagery during which you will stay focused on your topic and let your mind roll with every relevant idea revolving about this one topic or image.

_____

_____

_____

_____

_____

BE WILLING TO CHANGE YOUR VISION

Do not be afraid if your new ideas suggest you should change from your original idea. Should you recognize that you are changing, allow yourself to do that. Allow yourself to change your creative vision.

~ _For a long time, I had been planning all my choreography before arriving at rehearsals—always making up dances, working every step out in ad-_

vance. After a while, I began to feel that my work was too tight and too controlled. I wanted to work in a new way—to go into rehearsal cold, to be able to stand in front of my dancers and just see what would come, without a previously thought-out plan—but I was afraid to try. I feared that nothing would come and that I would freeze up in front of all of them. Finally, I asked one group of dancers if they would be willing to come work with me, not promising them that a dance or a concert would come of it. Seven volunteered to work with me. As I stood in front of them, trying to let go of my fear and letting my body move and respond to the moment, lo and behold, I began to move with great spontaneity and excitement. The movements were interesting and new, and I liked what was coming out of me. In fact, it did turn into a good dance that I called Currents, *and that experience changed forever the way I worked and the kinds of dances that have since come out of me. Ever since then, I have been a much more spontaneous choreographer, willing to intermingle my energies with the moment of creation in the space with the dancers with whom I am working. This method is more fun and lively, even though it is still full of risk for me. Because of that dare that I gave myself, my dances have been richer, more interesting, and more successful. And, in contrast to my deepest, previous fear that no ideas would come to me in this process, instead in working in this spontaneous way, I have* NEVER *drawn a blank in rehearsal.* (L.B.)

ACTION 5: Write down and describe your various visions of your creative goals and work, and note the changes that may have occurred over time. Describe how such changes have affected your life and work.

_____

_____

_____

_____

_____

~ *Several of my books have been forming in my mind for years before I could finally settle down to write them. I keep imagining different versions and drafting various plans. Over time, my ideas for the way they should be have changed; and, usually, it seems that the long period of time between the first idea of the work and its eventual, sometimes very different manifestation made it a much more interesting work than I had first imagined.* (L.C.)

IMAGINING THE CREATIVE ACT IN ALL YOUR LIFE

"Imagining the Creative Act" can work for anything you confront in your life—from deciding how to live your daily life, to how to work on others' projects, or how to set other directions in your life. You can use this process every day of your life.

~ *When I bought my new house in Miami, it was a wreck. I literally had to walk through debris on the floor. Everything was trashed, but I was able to see the potential when I looked at it. I could imagine what it would be like when I fixed it up. Now my friends can't fathom how I could see that originally and was able to make something out of such a mess.* (L.B.)

~ *It's the same for me whenever I prepare to decorate an interior space— like my house, a room, or my office. I first sit and look at the space and then look at everything I think would be appropriate in that space. I then envision the entire space decorated as I would like, imagining where every item will go, all before I begin to hang a single painting or move a piece of furniture. It works so well that some friends of mine have had me decorate their houses and apartments, and, in their cases, I do the same—first look at everything they have, then imagine the space and, after envisioning the scene, then decorate their space to fit their tastes and possessions.* (L.C.)

~ *That reminds me of when I saw this piece of sculpture I really wanted, and I went into my imagination and visualized my whole house to see exactly where it might fit. It didn't—so I did not buy it.* (L.B.)

~ *Before planting some new trees and shrubbery in my garden, I first spent a period of time looking out at the view as it was from different angles, from different places, at various hours of the day, and then I imagined what I wanted to see there on the horizon. It was only after I had the whole vision for the placement that I then had the trees and bushes planted exactly as I had seen the new view of my garden in my mind's eye.* (L.C.)

~ *When I get ready to teach a class, I go into a kind of meditative imaginary space and envision the students I'm going to teach. And in this imagining, it comes to me what they need to learn. That's why my first class—before I know the students—is always so difficult because I don't yet know them.* (L.B.)

~ *I do that, too, when I am preparing to give a speech or conduct a seminar in some new place. First of all, in advance, just as I teach in my public speaking classes, I try to get an idea of who will be in the audience, imagine their expectations, and I always try to see the actual site—the room or the auditorium—and imagine performing, speaking there. Then, as I prepare my speech—practicing out loud or in my mind—I envision actually delivering it. Interestingly, now that I think about it, this imagining the act prior to the live event serves as a dress rehearsal and makes the actual performance flow better. Of course, I'm sure you do this all the time with preparing for your dance performances. Imagining the creative act is definitely part of the creation.* (L.C.)

~ *That's absolutely right. You know, Liz, I realize that in my whole life, I spend a lot of time imagining what something will be like before doing it—whether it's deciding to accept a party invitation or take a trip. Now it's almost that every time before I take any action, I have a daydream about it. And that's how I create my environment, my classes, and my life.* (L.B.)

~ *I can remember when I wanted to envision myself in a particular job I was offered. So I meditated and could see all the things that I could do in this job that I could not see just from the job description. And, then, I real-*

ized this was the right job for me, and I could be the creative person I wanted to be in it. I decided then and there to accept it. Then, of course, I had to imagine how to make it happen—get everything in place, make all the necessary changes to be able to move in the new direction. I think we have to do this kind of advance imagining all the time throughout our lives. (L.C.)

Keys

ℂ *Before bringing your creative expression into a form, you must first envision it in your mind's eye.*

ℂ *Envisioning is the time for your great dreaming and your vivid imaginings.*

ℂ *Exploring the unknown and taking risks in imagination will help bring you to unlocking the door of creative action.*

~~~~~~~~~~~~~~~~~~~~~~~~~~~~~~~~~~~~~

Getting It out of Your Head

Getting it out of your head" is bringing your creative ideas into a form. And this first form for ALL endeavors will be graphic in some way—in other words, writing, sketching, outlining, drawing, or engraving. This activity—putting your idea into a graphic form—is an essential step in the creative process.

PREPARING TO PUT YOUR IDEAS INTO A GRAPHIC FORM

This chapter describes the critical step of bringing your ideas into form—getting them out of your head and onto paper. No matter what the art form is, the creative act requires some kind of graphic rendering. It's the connective tissue between the mind and the product. Notebooks of artists of all kinds fill our libraries. Intriguing us with these almost unintelligible notes, sketches, plans, and designs, they provide us with universal evidence of this vital intermediary step in the creative process.

The first step to bringing a vision to reality is this rendering, sketching, writing, drawing, drafting, outlining, designing, planning in some graphic style. It will probably be a mixture of all these graphic forms. Until you do this step, you have not really made an outward expression of your vision. This can be very frightening and frustrating because you think you can't possibly make it like the vision in your head. But now you must take your ideas from your head, from your brain's vision, and put them down if you wish to be creative.

It is very likely that your internal and external critics will show up at any number of junctures during this process. Whenever they do, please refer to the section on "Banishing Your Internal and External Critics" on page 96.

~ Because I know that this is such a critical point in creating whatever work or project—to concentrate exclusively on the matter at hand, to focus laser-like on bringing out all my ideas on this one topic—I cut myself off from all other activities and often ritualize it by writing first in my journal about going through the process, about entering the state. It is so critical that my mind flows freely and strongly on one subject that I have to enter an almost trance-like state, get into what is often also called the zone. (L.C.)

ACTION 1: Prepare yourself for this exciting moment. This is your first attempt at bringing your ideas into reality. Here you will make your first graphic representation of what you have been envisioning in your mind's eye, your dreams, your head.

Step 1: Set aside a specific amount of time during which you will focus exclusively on forming your ideas.
Step 2: Return to a creative space of solitude.
Step 3: Perform some sort of initial ritual to represent your commitment to bringing your vision into form.
Step 4: Take five to ten deep breaths that will help center you and oxygenate your body to prepare you for the beginning of your great work.

PUTTING YOUR IDEAS INTO GRAPHIC FORM

Now is the time to put down in some graphic form everything you know, everything you have planned about your work. This is one of the times when you get the pay-off for all the hard work. If you ever doubted why one pursues the often lonely road to creative expression, it is at this moment of birthing that you should begin to be convinced of the joys, the almost orgasmic experience of creation. This should be a time of great exhilaration and delirium. It seems as if you are working in a frenzy and there is not enough time to get it all out the way you have imagined it. You are afraid to stop for fear it might disappear. It can feel like an aphrodisiac. Enjoy this high moment—one of the most fulfilling you can ever have in life.

It is at this point that everything that is internalized about a particular imagined, creative act is now externalized in a plan, a mapping out of the vision.

~ What I always first do when I am finally ready to bring my ideas for any project out of my head—whether it's for a book, a course, a speech, a business or strategic plan—is to jot every idea down as fast as it comes, almost like throwing up without any control over what comes out—without editing, usually without writing sentences, without taking time to write explanations or elaborations, just notes. Often I try to put them on one or only a few pieces of paper, and they do not often come out in an order—that's not important at this point. The important thing, I believe, is simply to get everything out of my head without stopping to think long about one particular thought, or else I'll get bogged down on one and lose the moving train of thought that allows everything to roll out freely. Only afterwards do I begin to order my ideas, make formal outlines, write longer explanations, elaborate on the first thoughts. This is always very exciting, and I make every effort to stay totally focused and get the first throwing up of the ideas all done, down on paper, in one sitting. (L.C.)

ACTION 2: Put down on paper (or in your journal) everything you know about your vision. Put it down in any graphic form or forms you wish. Make notes, maps, sketches, diagrams, as they come to you. At this point, do not edit your notes and markings. Just throw pictures, ideas, and words on the paper without any order.

_____

_____

_____

_____

_____

This is a very high time for the creative person. You may feel as if you're standing in the middle of a waterfall or a big avalanche. You may lose track of all time as you rush to get your ideas out onto paper. This is also one of the times that is often described as the "aha!" experience when things seem to be clear and you will be at one with the universe as your own ideas burst forth into reality.

Start right now on this beautifully blank page . . .

ACTION 3: CELEBRATE this translation of your vision into reality. Do something physical. Or perform a ritual. Treat yourself to something special, like a walk or a massage. Share it with an imaginary friend. Or, if you have been communicating with one trusted person that you are engaged in a special creative project, then confide in that person that you have finally brought your idea out of your head into some kind of form onto paper. You need not reveal the details. And then prepare to go back to the work.

WARNING: After this initial outpouring of everything in your head about this project, you may have the feeling of being spent. At the same time that you have felt exhilaration, you may also soon feel exhausted. You have just experienced a great high. Be prepared to endure this and move on to the next step.

WARNING: After the elation, the hard work will begin again. Initially, it will all seem clear to you. But the next morning, after the celebration, you might think you have a great mess on your hands and no solution in sight for how to organize your ideas into a single creative form. This is the normal unfolding of the creative process. Do not despair. You will now begin the organizing and forming of your ideas.

~ *After I paint the first quick strokes, outlining shapes and dabbing in colors, I stop, leave the canvas on the easel, and walk away. Every time I pass by the canvas, I look at it anew and begin to envision where I will go next with the work once I return to painting.* (K.H.)

~ *Whenever I brainstorm about my ideas for a new marketing plan and have jotted down every notion I can think of, I then leave it for a while and let it sit before trying to organize them into a cohesive proposal. Even when it seems chaotic and unclear, I wait a period of time before returning to put order to my plan. I used to worry that I wasn't producing the plan fast enough and would push myself to continue straight from the brainstorming.*

Now, instead of beating myself up because the plan did not emerge in perfect organization from my head, I know that this hiatus—however short, just letting it sit overnight—really helps clarify my ideas, and then it becomes easier to approach the jumble and put the puzzle together. (C.K.)

ORGANIZING YOUR IDEAS

Begin to organize your project, to make the plan and ultimately the outline or model or *maquette* of your project. Now that you have gathered your notes and scribblings, you are ready to begin organizing your ideas into more of a form. You may need a number of sessions, even sometimes months or years, to determine the final plan for a creative work. Many great artists take years to organize and plan their great works.

You must be prepared to feel totally overwhelmed with the enormousness of the task in front of you. In looking at the grand picture, begin to see the details that need to be considered. We suggest that you break your project down into bits and pieces, into small sections. You might also want to put them on separate cards or pieces of paper, and then spread them out in front of you so that you can visually and physically begin to organize your whole together with all its parts.

~ When I am creating a new work, I break the whole idea into parts, whether I am choreographing a dance or putting a series of poems together. I divide the project into smaller ideas and put them on 3 x 5 cards in order that I can re-arrange them until I find the proper order of how I want to present my work. It also makes the large, often initially insurmountable-seeming task become manageable and possible for me. I can deal with little bites much better than with a great big chunk. (L.B.)

Play with different possibilities. Re-arrange structures and outlines. Envision and dream the whole and the parts. At this point you are using both the creative, intuitive side of your brain and also the rational, logical side. The latter is important for organizing your work, but you need to be careful not to give up your creative, intuitive ways of approaching your work.

ACTION 4: Begin the process of organizing all your ideas for this work. Try to determine an order for all the ideas you have gathered for this particular creative work.

_____

_____

_____

_____

_____

~ *This is when I usually start transferring the notes to other pages and scratching each off from the original paper as I put it under a heading on this more organized page. Often I will even begin by taking scissors and cutting each different notation from the original page and laying them out to find an order. I find that the mechanical act stimulates the mental process of organizing.* (L.C.)

EMBELLISHING

You have your specific idea. You have begun to order it. You are focused. Now it is time to embellish it, to fill in the blanks, to add or subtract ideas that you might have left out before. It is very important to remember to continue taking this process of refinement forward into even the smallest parts of your project in order that you are not overwhelmed by the whole. After all, it is in the details that your work is most compellingly and uniquely your expression. At the same time, it is critical that you always return to your creative space as you work through your entire project. Here it is very important to let your mind be free again and daydream, re-envision, imagine what else is needed.

~ *I always use the daydreaming process to take my projects forward. Whether I am planning a class, decorating a room, or looking to see where my next rehearsal must go, I get in a sort of trance and let myself open up to my imaginings and daydreams. I allow my mind to roam freely until I am presented with solutions and ways to go forward. This is how I embellish my initial plan whenever that is necessary.* (L.B.)

ACTION 5: Embellish the different parts of your plan. Fill in the blanks, so to speak, of every aspect of the whole plan.

_____

_____

_____

_____

_____

REFINING

After embellishing your plan, stop and re-examine your original plan, your outline, to see if there's anything extraneous, superfluous, unrelated to the intention of the work. This again is a critical step in planning the work before you finally begin to put it down in the form you wish it to become.

ACTION 6: Refine your plan in order that you have a model to follow as perfectly as is possible.

~ *Depending on the work, I find that this step of refining can sometimes take hours, in some projects even years, and I have to prepare myself for allowing the different stages of my creative organization and endeavor to go through different lengths of time for this refining germination.* (L.C.)

WARNING: Your great enthusiasm may push you to want to share your ideas at this moment. Do not do it at this point in your creative outpouring. Refrain from this strong temptation to share too much about your work and the details of your ideas with someone else before they are finished. Instead, wait until you have completed your work, and then you can and, ultimately, must share it, if it is to be a fully completed creative work.

~ *Of course, there are times when it helps to share your ideas and get feedback. In a lot of work, you have to do that all the time, as part of a work team, and it's extremely beneficial. The more you discuss an idea, the more developed it becomes, growing because of others' comments and questions.* (K.H.)

~ *It depends upon the type of work. Yet, even in most fields of creative endeavor, at this stage, this step, of just throwing out your ideas—before actually beginning to put them into a form, it seems it's a good idea to be careful not to share much. What happens to most people is that we get really excited about some ideas and then run and tell others, and, then, in the telling, the whole idea gets dissipated and, ultimately, lost.* (L.C.)

~ *But then, again, using a trusted friend or colleague as a sounding board for your ideas can prove very helpful in advancing and forming the plan for your work. I think it has to be a case-by-case decision; but, of course, you should be careful in selecting the appropriate person or people with whom to share. But I say, you need to share your ideas sometimes at this stage.* (K.H.)

~ *I would add, though, that this danger of dissipation includes the fact that sometime in the telling of the early ideas, the creative person ends up not pursuing or not finishing a project because of feeling it's already been made—by telling it. But, in fact, it never happened. The work was never created because it "got lost in the telling."* (L.C.)

~ *I have shared dances before they were finished and did not get the response that I was hoping for and then became very depressed and thrown off course.*

It caused me to doubt my vision of the work and even to question my whole reason for doing what I do. After all, dance is very ephemeral, and there is not much reward except in the doing of it—the dancing itself. My dancers affect me if they do not like the movement that I give them. If the dance does not move enough, they are often bored and do not feel physically challenged. Such reactions are very upsetting to me because I want to please my dancers. Obviously, the more they like doing it, the more cooperative they will be in rehearsal. If I want to try something with less movement in it, perhaps try something more theatrical or moody, it is often very difficult to get the dancers to want to follow my vision. At such times I have to work really hard not to be affected adversely by negative vibes my dancers might give off during rehearsal. I have to carry on with my vision of the finished created work. (L.B.)

WARNING: Why should you not share this wonderful birthing? Your work is not ready, and you may be disappointed by the reaction of anyone with whom you choose to share your first outpouring of ideas for your creative project.

~ As a choreographer, there are always people observing my work, whether it is the dancers who are working with me or the other people who hang around the dance studio. It is extremely difficult to stay focused on one's task, particularly if I am trying something new. I used to get very nervous that I was being judged. I used to want my dance to look wonderful right away in case anyone happened by, even though I knew the process of perfecting the choreography and the performance always takes weeks and sometimes months before the completed work is performed. I was being driven crazy by my own internal voices putting imaginary judgments in the mouths of people who just happened to pass by while the creation of the work was in progress. Eventually, however, I learned that I was my own judge and critic, that no one else could judge my art, my actions, or my choices. Life and making art have become much easier for me since I have been able to adopt and apply that attitude. (L.B.)

WARNING: Jealousy and envy on others' parts can also, unfortunately, at times lead to theft of ideas. You must finish the process and take it to fruition with a completed work before you begin to share it.

~ *I was working on a script that I was creating off some poetry that I had written. I was working out of town with a group of dancers who also had a lot of acting experience. Wanting to try the script out since I had never done anything like this before, I devoted an entire rehearsal to it. As it was successful and I felt the project had potential, I then tucked it away for use at some future time. A year later, I returned to the town and learned that one of the dancers who had worked with me was putting on her own concert. The flyers plastered all over the town sent me into shock—the concert's title was the very same title as my script that we had worked on the previous year. Stunned that the other dancer had stolen my title, I realized the danger of sharing any project before you are ready to proceed.* (L.B.)

~ *I sent my proposal off to an agent, and then I didn't hear back for ages. Finally, I contacted the agent, who said there was no interest in my proposal. Although I had thought it was a really exciting and timely idea, I became discouraged and did not send it immediately to another agent, as I think I should have. A couple of years later, as I was browsing through books in an airport, I was astonished to find a book with a similar title to the one I'd proposed and, inside, one page after another were my own words.* (A.R.)

BANISHING YOUR INTERNAL AND EXTERNAL CRITICS

It is important through all of this to tell your internal and external critics to leave you alone. If you allow any in at all, you run the risk of being stopped completely in your tracks. As tempting as it will be to share your project and your ideas with others, it is highly recommended that you do not share anything until you have completed your project to the best of your ability. When you share prematurely, the energy of the project can get dissipated and you might lose your creative thrust. In addition, because you are in a very sensitive and vulnerable place as you prepare for your creative expression, your expectations of how it will be received might not be met and might be taken by you as critical and unenthusiastic. So it is advisable not to open yourself up to any kind of criticism or scrutiny.

~ *At the end of my dance* Currents, *and long before we had easy access to video cameras, someone made a film of the performance and showed it to the dancers. I was appalled at watching myself. All I could see were what I viewed as my faults. I had such an idealized image of how I and the dance should look. On seeing the film, I was so critical of myself that I refused to perform for some time after that. It took me two full years to come to terms with who I really was and to begin again to share with my audiences my gifts of performing.* (L.B.)

ACTION 7: List all the internal and external critics who might block your creative progress.

_____

_____

_____

_____

_____

Then put the list in a box or drawer, and put it away, out of sight and out of your mind. Tell yourself you will deal with them another day, if ever. Or you might even choose to burn your list and ritualistically destroy your critics forever. If they keep returning to bother and distract you, you will want to examine them to see why it is they have such an effect on you and the progress of your work. Ideally, you will eventually be able to take advantage of your blocks and critics—to put them to use in your creative work, to incorporate them into the developmental process.

You are now ready to concretize your ideas, to bring your ideas into a new, whole, creative reality. Be sure you know everything you need to know about your idea before you make the final creative act—the final, exciting moment of birth.

Key

    Getting your ideas out of your head is putting your creativity into form.

~~~~~~~~~~~~~~~~~~~~~~~~~~~~~~~~~

Creating the Work

H ere you are poised with your creative plan, initial sketches and/or notes, and first outpourings. Now you are ready to quit planning and start creating the full work. This is the time for turning your creative work into its finished form.

MAKE IT! DO IT! CREATE YOUR WORK!

You may think it has taken a long time to get here, but all this groundwork will make the creativity flow faster now. Even artists who say they had a moment of inspiration and sat down and did it are forgetting the whole long creative process that brought them to that point. They may have been unconscious of all the preliminary steps. As you become a more accomplished, more creative person, you, too, will do the first seven steps of this creative process almost unconsciously.

This chapter is about moving on to the next stage—putting the ideas and plans into the finished form. This is the beginning of the final work of creation.

Each creation has its own highs and its own hazards. Some come out easily, some with great difficulty. There is no predicting whether you will run into snags or smooth sailing.

No matter what, don't give up!

Enjoy this rare moment of creation, a high like no other. This is the most exciting time. Be fearless. Let it flow. Let it all come out. It can actually be orgasmic. Don't miss this fearsome, fabulous moment.

ACTION 1: Note here or in your journal that you are now about to complete the final act of creating your work.

_____

_____

_____

_____

_____

This formally written acknowledgment, the statement of your intention, serves an important purpose in encouraging you to move forward. This is one of the most difficult moments of all in the creative process, and you will need all the back-up of "intentionality" for yourself. In this writing, describe how you feel and what you expect to accomplish and when. Noting this moment in this way serves as a kind of ritual consecration of this final act of creation.

SET THE SCENE

Try to be as creative as possible in setting the scene for your work. This also reflects your uniqueness. Make your whole creative space—physical and mental—represent your individuality. This is YOUR work. Do it your own way. There are no prescriptions, only guidelines.

~ *For some time I felt as if I was not getting anything creative done anymore. I had been feeling that I needed a different space in which to work because my office had become cluttered with too many things, bills to be paid, school work, storage items. The only extra space was a guest room that most of the time was empty, just waiting for company, and stored in my garage was an old dining room table that I was not using. So I brought the old table into the unoccupied guest room and set it under the window with its wonderful view of the neighbor's trees. I dedicated this table to only one project at a time. It has become a very special place for me. It is a clear space with nothing on it except when I bring a particular project to it, whether it is my latest book, my taxes, or student papers for grading. When the project is completed, I clear the table, making it ready for the next project. This has worked very well for me, and I have become much more productive. Whenever I have house guests, the table gets a lovely bowl of flowers on it, and, of course, is off limits to me and my work-projects while they are staying there.* (L.B.)

ACTION 2: Set the scene for making your ideas a creative reality. You are actually beginning a kind of meditation—your creative practice.

Step 1: Set aside a specific time for your work. This could mean spending an hour on it each day or going away for a weekend. It may take you a summer or a year. But you must find your own work pattern.

Step 2: Again, choose an appropriate space where you will be undisturbed by telephones and people, completely undistracted, in a safe location that's conducive to total solitude, ideally an isolated place—a room in your house, a grove in the woods, some hideaway. If this space for some reason does not feel right for you to do your work, then perhaps you will need to move yourself to another area which is more conducive to encouraging your creativity.

Step 3: Bring together whatever equipment you may need for what you've chosen to create. A dancer needs enough space. A painter needs paints, brushes, and canvas. A writer needs notebooks and/or a computer. A businessperson needs a worktable or a laptop.

Step 4: Once you are ready to begin, we suggest that you separate yourself from your everyday life by performing some kind of ritual—such as saying a mantra about your uniqueness, lighting a candle, saying some sort of prayer or incantation, burning incense, or playing music. (Some artists have been known to use drugs or to drink alcohol to accelerate their creative process and also to overcome their inhibitions. But we do not advise taking any of these external stimulants because, in the long run, these can destroy your creativity and even ultimately take away your very life.)

Step 5: Take three to five deep breaths to center your thoughts and oxygenate your body as you now begin the final creation of your great work.

Every time you return to the same space where you have invested your creative energy, it will become easier for you to connect, to get into your creative flow, and to begin your work. It is as if every time you visit this space, you are leaving a layer of your most creative self there and you will become eager to return. You are actually creating a sacred space for yourself. It becomes a place of personal power, your place for creativity.

SELF-DISCIPLINE

Begin your sculpture, poem, dance, business plan, painting, marketing strategy, house decoration, design, book, garden landscaping. This act requires the greatest self-discipline of all. You make yourself do it, whatever that requires—without interruption. It may or may not flow effortlessly, but at this point you can't give up. Remember that, while it's possible to be planning more than one work at a time, you can actually create only one work at any particular moment in time.

~ *Don't give me that talent thing. It's tenacity, as many others have observed. In sculpting, it's working over and over again. But, actually, I think tenaciousness is necessary in any kind of serious work, artistic or otherwise. I believe that good creative work takes a certain compulsivity.* (M.C.)

All your preparatory work will lead you into your creation. Don't be intellectual about it. You must allow your work to flow, without judgment. This is not the time to edit or break it. Don't let your inner (or outer) critic, judge, editor, step in here. If they appear, simply tell them to "GO AWAY!" Do it. (This really works.)

~ *The only solution I've ever found if I really want to do my best creative work is to cut myself off from all else during a period of time. My advice is simple: "Lock yourself in your house until it's done!" That is the only way.* (L.S.)

~ *Once I followed that advice and "locked" myself onto my property for a week—no running errands, no exercising outside my grounds, no meetings, few phone calls, no e-mail—and I managed to create a major piece of work in that time. It worked.* (E.C.)

ACTION 3: Begin the process. Take the first step. Take brush to canvas. Write the first sentence. Note the first note of music. Draw the first line. Chisel the first chip of the stone. Engrave the first mark.

~ *No matter what, the first thing I do on entering my studio is pick up a brush and paint anything, run it across the canvas. That always forces me to get started.* (S.E.)

STAY WITH THE FLOW

Focus.

Stay with it.

Stay with the flow.

Keep your momentum—for at least a few hours.

We recommend that you set time limits for each work session. No matter how you plan to complete your work—whether in a short period of time with deadlines or over a longer period of time—you should plan that your breaks are only intermittent and that during those breaks you do not get too far away from focusing on your work.

~ *In sculpting, you have to get the essence of life into your work. You've got to punch life into it. You have to stay with it, thinking about it all the time, even when your model is gone. It's the eye and the expression that you have to think through and capture, the essence of the living person or animal you're trying to replicate. It's a lot of work. You keep looking at it— adding and subtracting clay—until it happens. You have to be tenacious.* (M.C.)

~ *Among the most creatively productive times of my life were the three summers when I immersed myself so completely in my writing projects that I never wore a watch and just wrote, slept, ate, walked, swam, played with my cats, and talked with only a very few truly supportive friends. During the most intense and best periods of those summers, I just slept until I woke up, then wrote some more, took a break, wrote again, fell asleep when I was tired. There was no sense of time, the days and nights just rolling with the flow of the work. They were what I call delicious times—wonderful periods of about two months each, during which I finished a couple of books—and, even though at first it had been hard to get into the immersion, at the end, I hated having to return to the "real world" at the end of the summer. It was like being in a cocoon in paradise.* (L.C.)

ACTION 4: Commit yourself to stay a specific amount of time to work on your project. Do not wait for the muse. Even if you just stare into space, schedule yourself to stay for certain lengths of time with your project in each session.

~ *My mother wrote children's stories. But because she had a lot of children herself, it was always difficult for her to find the time. Finally, she would get herself into such a state of worry about her deadlines that she would quite literally disappear for several days, going into her writing room and spinning out her tales. Fortunately, my father was very supportive of her work, and he would prepare food for her that we children would then carry up to her room and leave outside her door. She would re-emerge, happily, after a few days and another storybook written. That was the only way she could get her work done, just bury herself in it.* (L.P.)

~ *A time in my life when I accomplished a great deal creatively was when I took several weeks out of my regular schedule—basically, my vacation time —and then focused exclusively on writing my book proposal and my business plan. During that period, I did nothing else, and I followed somewhat flexible daily schedules I'd set for myself. It was most invigorating, and I accomplished all the tasks I'd set for myself.* (E.E.)

~ *The truth of the matter about my writing romance novels is that I have to stay up very late and get up very early if I'm ever to finish as well as hold a full-time office job, be a wife, and be a mother to two young children. I'm lucky to have a very encouraging husband who also gives me time on weekends.* (K.C.)

If this is your first project, do not take on too much. Try writing a short story, not a novel. Make a three-minute dance, not one that lasts half an hour. Break that business plan down into one-year segments. Write a one-act play. In other words, do not take on too big or too complex an idea at the beginning. Otherwise, you may become quickly discouraged and frustrated and give up before you have allowed yourself to get into your creative potential.

TAKE A BREAK!

Some time away from the work itself, however, can bring you a fresh perspective and will more clearly direct you in the refinement of your work. If you are able to come to the work anew and fresh each time, you can often see more clearly how the work needs to develop. Also, as we have noted earlier, it is during breaks that you may get your best ideas after you have done a lot of work on a particular project. So, after productive periods of work, do let yourself relax and take breaks for revitalization.

~ *Once I have begun my work, anytime I go away from it, either take a walk or sleep on it, I always come back with a fresh perspective.* (L.B.)

~ *My most creative ideas often come immediately after taking a nap. In fact, whenever I lie down—take a break in my work—the ideas just flow out. I always keep a pad with me wherever I take a nap.* (M.W.)

Give yourself permission to stop the process and go away from it for a while. You will have to recognize that the idea of time is never the same in any creative work, and there is usually no way to gauge exactly how much time a particular work will take. But every time you return after being away from it for a while, it is advisable to go through the ritualistic steps of setting the scene and getting back into it.

~ *One of the best times of creative work I ever had was when I required myself to stick to a schedule, which I set each night before, of sitting at my work for several hours at a time before getting up and breaking. The rough daily time-table included breaks in between the work periods. But, then, sometimes when I would really get on a roll, I would not get up for many hours, and those work periods flowed into each other. After such an intense session, I would then leave the house, get completely away from my work— sometimes go out into some beautiful natural setting to unwind from the exciting creative work or go sit in a café or take a swim or a walk. During that time, I removed myself, yet my mind was still on the project, coming up with new ideas. No matter where I went following such intense work periods, I always came up with fresh ways of thinking that put me straight into the next phase of the creative work when I returned to it after a few hours or so.* (L.C.)

ACTION 5: Observe what happens in your breaks from your work. Take note of how you spend your breaks and if and when you have problem-solving or other creative ideas during or immediately after those times. Write about how and when the ideas come to you then.

_____

_____

_____

_____

_____

KEEP IT A SECRET!

Keep your work a secret until it is completed and fully ready to be shared. This is a personal and private act between you and yourself. And, indeed, it can be a dangerous risk to share it prematurely, even with someone who loves you. Time and again, people's creative work comes to a complete halt because someone has criticized it before it could be born. Some criticism is well-intentioned, of course, but even that does not help in the beginning. Lots of criticism from those who love you actually is sometimes intentionally destructive. They may be jealous of your focused purpose and the time it takes away from them. You cannot sabotage your work by sharing it before it's done. Guard it like your best-kept secret.

~ *It really depends on the kind of art it is. I mean you write novels, and I write poems. I can show a short poem to someone without risking losing it. Whereas if you shared your novel before you're ready, you run a risk.* (L.B.)

~ *I usually find that, until I feel it's ready to show, the best thing is just to say something vague and very general about it when people ask. Over the years, I've learned that the books and stories I end up writing are those that I didn't discuss much, at least as a book, until I could present them to someone else to see and read.* (L.C.)

~ *I disagree because I've found that it's really helpful to me being in a writing group and presenting my work for criticism as I go along.* (E.E.)

~ *Again, I think it depends upon the kind of work and the people you choose to share the work with as you go. It can be very helpful, and it can contribute very positively to the final product, particularly when you are developing a business idea within your own department or division. This kind of creativity often requires teamwork.* (K.H.)

~ *I think it also depends on both the type of work and your personality. I'm an extrovert, and my natural tendency is to talk about what I'm doing. I have to be careful about that. It's the problem we discussed earlier of the danger of the work being dissipated before it's finished.* (L.B.)

ACTION 6: Prepare a noncommittal answer (not a lie, but something vague and non-disclosing) that you will be able to give to people who constantly ask what you're doing, what you're working on, what it's about.

~ *For example, if you're writing a novel, you might simply answer that you're just working on a writing project. If they push you, then you might simply respond that it's about people in love.* (L.C.)

~ *If you're trying to paint a particular picture, you might say you're working on some painting exercises—"It's a new project I'm trying out. I can't talk about it now, but I'll let you know as soon as I come up with something I like."* (K.H.)

~ *Or, even better, "I've been reading this great new book that tells me not to talk about my work until it's done!"* (L.B.)

BEWARE OF THE PITFALLS

While you are engaged in the process of completing your creative work, you need to be prepared for a variety of pitfalls, or obstacles, that may throw you off course. Here are some of the kinds of pitfalls you might encounter:

- Realizing it is not going to come out the way you thought, planned, dreamed
- Getting stuck in the middle
- Being disappointed in your initial effort
- Being paralyzed by perfectionism
- Dealing with fears of success, failure, and/or change

It is Not Going to Come out the Way You Thought, Planned, Dreamed

Almost always when you try to bring your creative plan into reality, the work you actually produce does not match the vision you had for that work. This happens to all great artists and visionaries. It is a known fact about the creative process. Still it is extremely frustrating. When you experience this with your own work, do not become so frustrated that you cease to continue. Everyone experiences this. Just keep going anyway, and bring out your vision as best you can. Do not let your perfectionism get in the way.

~ *As a choreographer, I always dream of people flying and doing spectacular leaps and turns, hanging upside down in mid-air and doing other amazing, acrobatic feats. So I am almost always disappointed with my earthbound dancers. Now, however, with interactive video and digitalization of images, I guess that some of the wild ideas I have long had in my head might be possible. If not, I'll just keep dreaming and trying to make my creations as close as possible to my visions.* (L.B.)

What to Do When You Get Stuck

When you get stuck and nothing is flowing no matter how hard you try, stop there and go to another part of the work. Then return to the original point and begin again. If you keep getting stuck in one place, perhaps you need to re-think it. You may need to work on a smaller or a different part of it. You may even decide to find another place for your work. There are a number of reasons you may get stuck. Perhaps . . .

- You are too close to it emotionally.
- You missed a step in its planning.
- You have not done enough preparatory work for that part.
- There may be some aspect of it which you are avoiding.
- It may be so important to you that you want to make it perfect.
- There may be critical voices, inside and outside, stopping you from your work.
- New demands from other sources—work, personal, anything—have been placed on you.

Whatever it is, it may be important for you to re-examine yourself and the work, to figure out why you are stuck, in order to get around the blockage at that point. Again, the main point is to press on and not to give up the work because of being blocked at one or several places in the process.

What if You Are Disappointed with Your Initial Effort

If you are disappointed with your first creative work, if you feel it is not as spectacular as you had hoped: Do not give up. Keep at it. Later, after completing your first full draft or your initial output, then you can go back to it and re-work it. It is really important that you keep moving forward and not get bogged down in any editing or changing at this point. Take it all the way through to completion before thinking of changing it in any way.

~ In dance, it is a given that we work towards the finished product. The dance always comes out for me first as a sketch that I slowly fill in over time. Also, the dancers need time to perfect the movements that I have given them, and they have to learn to work together so that they work in ensemble, creating a cohesive whole. This is usually a six- to eight-week process. The dance rarely comes out the first time as I expected. I must get used to how long the process takes, even though I wish it would just come out quickly and perfectly right away. (L.B.)

Dangers of Perfectionism

There is no such thing as perfection. So you had better get rid of the word as soon as possible. Eradicate the word from your vocabulary. All you can do is the very best you can do. That is all anyone can do. And with that you must be satisfied.

Perfectionism is said to breed procrastination, which then leads to paralysis—and, hence, failure to begin and/or finish your creative work. Many creative people suffer from this debilitating syndrome.

~ This is where I get really bogged down. I keep trying to perfect an idea or a work, instead of just getting it out there, putting it out in the world.

I've observed that many prolific artists and creators of all kinds let perfectionism stall their work. Of course, this is not to say there's no need for some perfectionism. It's just a shame when one lets it stop the work from ever getting out to a wider audience. (L.C.)

More artists have lived in misery because they never lived up to their imagined goal of what perfection was. It is the greatest destroyer of happiness and fulfillment and pride in your work. So, if you want to be really miserable, keep holding your false notion of perfection. Instead, focus on doing your very best. This concept of perfectionism ties right into the idea of "not being good enough," which ties right in with the idea that "you yourself are not good enough." If this is where your creativity comes to a halt, it is probably time for you to look into your belief system about your "not being good enough." Until you get over that idea, it is doubtful that you will get over the idea that your work is "not good enough." Likewise, if you're given feedback that you're "not good enough," then you should question the source. You need to stand up and say, "I am good enough. And my work is good enough."

Fear of Success / Fear of Failure / Fear of Change

Many people get stopped by themselves in the process because they are consciously or unconsciously worried about what will happen to them if they proceed toward completing their creative work. This could take the form of fear of success or fear of failure or fear of change in general. This fear could also evidence itself in fearing the obligation toward the creation, in actually fearing the ownership of the work and what to do with it once it is completed. If you feel that any of these fears are impeding you and keeping you back from continuing on your creative process, you must strive to overcome them. They are actually very normal, and most people experience such fears in some ways throughout their creative journeys. The important thing here is that you are aware of them as potential impediments to fulfilling your creative potential.

ACTION 7: List all the pitfalls to which you are especially susceptible as you enter this most important phase of creating your work. Describe how they affect you and your work, and describe how you can minimize and possibly even circumvent them.

EDITING, CUTTING, RE-ARRANGING, RE-WORKING

After your initial output is complete, what's next?

Everyone works in different ways. Some people will be able to begin the editing process immediately. Others will set it aside in order to have fresh viewing eyes when they come back to it. Now, unless you feel the work is absolutely what you intend it to be, you will begin a process of editing, cutting, re-arranging, possibly re-working. Here you may want to embellish and add to the work.

ACTION 8: Edit your work. Cut it. Re-arrange it. Re-work it where necessary. You may have to repeat all these actions over and over again until you are satisfied.

WHEN IS IT READY FOR SHARING?

Whatever process you go through, at some point you will have the strong sense that this is enough, that it is complete.

TRUST that instinct. Your work is done and now ready to be shared.

ENJOY FULLY THIS MOMENT OF CREATIVE COMPLETION.

Keys

  At some point, you have to quit planning and do it.

  Turning your ideas into a form of creation requires immense self-discipline.

  Keep your ideas a secret until you have finished.

  Do not let criticism and perfectionism stop your creative process. Fears of success, failure, or change are pitfalls you must avoid.

  Enjoy fully this rare moment of creation.

KEY 9

~~~~~~~~~~~~~~~~~~~~~~~~~~~~~~~~~~

Sharing Your Creation

So you think you have finished?
You are never finished with your creative work until you have
shared it.

Once you have created your work—given birth to your baby—
you must take this essential next step: Share your creation with
others. Share it with the outside world.

THE FIRST SHARING

This chapter is about the critical and final step of the creative process, that is, sharing your work with others. It is not until this important step is taken that the cycle of the creative process is complete. For it is in this final step that a complete sense of sharing and
being heard and understood is realized by the creative person, the
creator. Sharing your act of creation gives you a sense of wholeness
and completion and empowers you as no other experience, even
though the risk of sharing is the most feared aspect of creativity.
This step also brings some of the greatest rewards.

Sharing, like all the other preceding steps, is both fearsome and
fabulous. The fulfillment of the creative act is not complete without sharing it. It is your unique contribution to the world. If you
had any questions about it before, realize now it is your human obligation to share your work. It is the sacred obligation of all people

to communicate their uniqueness through their creative endeavors.

Choose carefully the person or persons with whom you will do your first sharing. This first sharing can be very exhilarating and very frightening, both at the same time. Sometimes it can be so frightening that you just want to grab your work and run and hide. This fear is because you are sharing the most intimate parts of yourself—what truly represents who you really are. And, therefore, there's a built-in fear of rejection. This is also why it is so fabulous—because through this you reveal yourself. At the same time, you always grow as a result of bringing out your creative self.

To be successful in achieving your best work, you must put yourself through this scrutiny. In other words, you really have to put yourself through this in order to improve your work, but, more importantly, you will get the great high of touching other people with your creation. So choose wisely, think carefully about the person or persons with whom you want to do your first sharing. In the first sharing, you will get ideas about where it is not working, where the holes are and what needs fixing.

ACTION I: Name the person or persons with whom you wish first to share your work. Write here or in your journal about why you have chosen this particular person or persons. Writing about your reasons will help you deal with their first reactions.

Weigh the kinds of qualities this person should have before deciding to show her or him your work. You should respect and trust this person. Unfortunately, there is always a danger of your work being stolen if you are not careful about whom you show it to or with whom you discuss it before it is published or produced. The person with whom you choose first to share your work should be someone who:

- Will not make fun of it
- Will take you and your work seriously
- Will give you honest, careful, and considerate feedback
- Is willing to give you the time it will take to review the work and discuss it with you in the most thoughtful ways
- Makes you instinctively feel very safe

Consider carefully the criticism you receive. You will need to guard your own self-esteem and not let the criticism demolish you. At the same time, you cannot be so afraid of or completely resistant to criticism that you do not show your work to anyone.

MORE SHARING

After that first sharing, be sure to prepare your creative space again, going through the same rituals, to begin your changes and your editing. Do this sharing as many times as you think is necessary, but never give your power away. Keep your power and control over your creative work. Often people whose opinions you have sought will then take a vested interest in your work and begin to hound you about the progress of the changes they have suggested. You must be careful here to maintain your integrity about your own work.

~ *I find there are stages of sharing my work, and only I can be the judge of that—when and where and with whom and how. I have to be careful not to let others push me to share before I'm ready.* (E.K.)

ACTION 2: Share your work with other people, another audience.

GETTING AN ARTISTIC AGENT

Your creative work may be in a field that requires that you now find an agent to promote and sell your work in the outside world. If this is the case, then you should definitely obtain the services of such an agent or publicist or broker. For almost every field of creative expression, there are books and catalogues listing the various agents and the kind of work they represent. You might also want to consult friends and any other contacts you may have in your field to advise you about finding the right agent for you and your particular work. The important point here is that this is often the critical intermediate step for any creative person to get their work out into the world. You will have to pluck up your courage, once again, and begin the search for the right agent. And, again, as in creating the work itself, you cannot be put off by rejection. You may have to approach many agents before finding one who will agree to represent you or one with whom you feel comfortable and confident.

CHOOSING SOMEONE IN YOUR OWN FIELD

You may decide to choose someone within your own field, and then you will receive an expert's opinion. But, at the same time, you must also be prepared to take even that expert's criticism with consideration. You must be a careful judge of whatever criticism you receive.

~ *When I show a piece of choreography for the first time, it is very scary. I always enjoy watching my students experience this phenomenon for the first time and watching them change because of it. It is the most frightening yet, all at the same time, the most exhilarating experience a choreographer can have. And, instinctively, on showing it, I know where my dance is too slow and where there need to be changes. It is an amazing process. I do not know why or how it works, but it does. It is as if I become everyone in the audience, and I experience their experience with my work. That is why it often takes professional choreographers who have the opportunity to show their work many times, in many different places, sometimes a year or so to finalize a* dance. *They show it in its "work in progress" state for a while, constantly refining it. It takes the addition of the audience to work its way to completion, to its most "perfect" state in the eye of the choreographer. That is why, also, shows on New York's Broadway and in London's West End have long out-of-town trial runs in smaller, repertory theatres before at last coming up with the final, workable, successful product—the show for the Broadway stage.* (L.B.)

You may feel holes in the work as you watch your sharers experience it. This is a strange phenomenon. Your sharers do not have to tell you anything. As you share, you will instinctively know what needs to be changed. But you could receive resounding applause, even at this stage.

~ *When producing a piece or segment for a television news show, it is always part of the process to show the "work in progress" to other producers and editors, and then you get feedback on how it might be improved or even changed, if necessary. As the producer of the piece, I was always able to see where it needed work or change once I sat and watched that first viewing with the other judges.* (L.C.)

ACTION 3: Choose someone in your field, and share your work with that person(s).

~ *When my students complain about having to re-write papers, I always say how I, as a writer, am pleased when I have an editor. I find it a very satisfying experience to go through the editing process involved in getting a book published. Once the writer submits the manuscript to the editor/ publisher, that is only the beginning of a series of editorial steps. Finally, the author receives the benefit of another pair of eyes, those of a professional editor—a detached reader—and a not-detached marketer. Then the final editing process begins—discussing the work, receiving and incorporating the suggestions, re-writing, re-editing, going over the revised manuscript, re-writing and re-editing some more, then to copyediting and then detailed checking of copyediting, then review of the galleys before the book finally goes to press. And, after what always seems a long time, out it comes . . . your book. It's all very exciting.* (L.C.)

WHEN YOU KNOW YOUR WORK IS COMPLETE

When do you know that you are finally finished with this creative work? How do you know when it's right for you? This is something that you instinctively know.

You intuit that your creative work is done. No one can tell you.

~ *People are always asking when my particular creative work will be finished, and in the beginning, that's very threatening. Over time, though, I've learned to come up with answers, like, "Oh, thank you for your concern, but I'd rather not talk about it until I know it's really done."* (E.K.)

There is no formula. When you are done, you just know. You have nothing more to say. You see it, you read it, you observe it and you like it. You feel you have communicated all you can on this project in this particular form. You are thrilled by it just the way it is. Or you may just feel that this is as much time and energy as you wish to give to this project. You may just be ready to move on to another project.

~ *Sometimes, of course, there is the reality of the deadline, which requires that you must finish a work. In truth, as many creative people will say, the pressure of a deadline brings out one's most creative work. There are a lot of us in all fields who work best under deadline. Then, upon reaching the deadline, you know you are done because that sense of giving it your best almost magically coincides with the final time of finished production and sharing it with the world.* (L.C.)

ACTION 4: Write here or in your journal about how you know your work is complete. Describe your feelings about this sense of completion. Writing about it will always contribute to your sense of completion and also will contribute to your knowing in the future when other works are complete.

_____

_____

_____

_____

_____

~ *Once I was fortunate enough to be choreographing the work* The Unicorn, the Gorgon, and the Manticore *of the great composer Gian Carlo Menotti for a very special performance at the University of Michigan.* Unicorn *would be one half of the show, while Mr. Menotti would stage-direct a companion piece. As part of the project, the costumer, set designer, and I myself as the choreographer were all flown to New York to consult with the composer. It was a very special time, and Mr. Menotti gave me many insights into the meaning of* The Unicorn. *After the visit, I proceeded with rehearsals, which were fun and delightful, and I was having a great time making this piece. When I got to the final scene in which the Townspeople decide to descend upon the Poet's Castle to kill him because he has apparently destroyed the fantastical animals which he had been parading around the town square, they arrive only to find the Poet surrounded by these creatures, which were really his own creations. He had "killed" the creations of his fancy in order to move on to new directions, but the Townspeople had misunderstood what he was doing, and they wanted to destroy him. He confronts them with the question "How could I kill that which I have created? It is you, not I, that are the killers of a Poet's dream." And at the very end, the Poet dies in the arms of his creations. It was a beautiful ending, and I was having great difficulty finding how to complete it. I was in rehearsal with the Poet and the three animals, and, finally, it came to me what must happen. I showed the dancers what to do, and I went to the far end of the studio to watch this last scene unfold in front of me. As I watched it, I knew it was right, and I wept from my own depths. I knew that I had captured the essence of the piece. I was fulfilled. And Menotti loved it.* (L.B.)

SHARING YOUR WORK WITH THE WORLD

Once you feel you are done, then let it go. But do not put it in the closet and hide it away. Sharing it with only a few people is not sufficient. We urge you now to find ways to get your creative work out to the widest audience possible.

~ *I never feel that my work is complete until I share it. Whether it is a dance on a stage with an audience, a poem that I read to my daughter over the phone, or photographs that I frame and hang on my wall or give as gifts or sell, it is that sharing that I think puts my essence into the world. It is as if I am sharing an intimate part of myself with my friends, my family, and even the world. This seems very important to my well-being.* (L.B.)

~ *There is the most incredible feeling of satisfaction to hold your work, in the case of a writer—to see and hold your published book or article—or to see your work, like a video production, or to hear it, or to experience it as it's performed with an audience. These feelings are indescribably powerful.* (L.C.)

There is an amazing sense of acknowledgment of your creative activity once you have shared it, once you have put it out into the world.

Your creative work has its own life.

Your creative work is no longer yours.

Your creative work belongs to the world.

Connecting to Creativity ~

ACTION 5: Share your work with the outside world. Get it out there. Get it into the public realm.

Congratulations!

Keys

  Once you have created your work, you must share your creation with others—share it with the outside world.

  Your initial sharings improve your work and bring it to completion.

~~~~~~~~~~~~~~~~~~~~~~~~~~~~~~~~~~~~~

Post-creation and Beginning Again

When it is over, when you have completed and shared your work of creativity, you might experience a kind of postpartum depression and, possibly, complete exhaustion. You must give yourself the necessary recovery time. Do not beat yourself up for feeling this way. When the work is complete, you will probably feel like collapsing. You might feel lost, depressed, and convinced that no one understands you and your work. Prepare your nearest and dearest for your blues.

THE POST–CREATIVE ACT BLUES

Why do you feel this way? It is because you have just put a major part of your focus on fulfilling and completing this project. You have been totally absorbed by this for a while. Probably every waking moment has been devoted in some way to this creation. Once it is complete, it is done. And for a time, there is a large hole left in your life. You may wander around feeling you have no purpose, not knowing what to do with your time.

Connecting to Creativity ~

ACTION 1: Write here or in your journal about how you feel once your work has been shared and is completely behind you. Describe in detail your feelings, and consider them for future reference.

_____

_____

_____

_____

_____

Rather than despairing over being in this state of post-creative blues, you can convert this situation into what you already know is the positive, creative state of staring into space and doing nothing in order to find new ideas for your next project. Many artists and creative people circumvent this dilemma by already having new projects planned to begin as soon as they finish one. Although this way of working may eventually lead to burn-out, it does catapult you back into another gestation stage.

~ *Whenever I finish a dance, when I put the last movement on the dancers, and I know that I have reached the end, I am elated. It is a joy like no other. I feel free. I feel bubbly as champagne. I feel on top of the world. It is always a good day. I feel relieved, spent, and fulfilled. Sometimes I am ready to delve into another project. But more often than not, I want to do other things for a while, other kinds of activities and tasks that I have put off during the great intense time of the making of the new creation. We all react differently at the end. I know many who go right into another project in order not to feel the emptiness. My daughter, who is a visual artist, always calls me at the end of a big project, relating to me how empty and tired she feels and that she doesn't know what is wrong with her. I always must remind her about the depletion after the great expenditure of energy during the creative process.* (L.B.)

~ Key 10 Post-creation and Beginning Again

You must allow yourself now, once again, to stare into space BIGTIME.

~ *After completing a work, I then have to return and face the reality of the so-called "real-life pressures." Then, after dealing with them, I have to do something that is really mindless for a while before I can jump into my next big project. And, often, I then have to face the fact that I need to earn some more money. So I quickly go and get a seemingly mindless job to tide me over for the next creative immersion when I then drop out of the world again.* (E.K.)

Some creative people, however, already are into a new project before they complete the current one. This becomes a useful way to avoid the downtime after completion of one project. But you can do this for just so long before the need for germination sets in, and you will find yourself devoid of ideas and as if you have nothing more to say. Experience this downtime. It will allow the new creative work to germinate.

~ *Usually when I finish some big work, I then like to return in a big way to a very sociable world, to human society. In intermingling and socializing, which I often have had to cut out of my life during the most intensely creative times, I then get a shot from that side of my life that I've not enjoyed for a while. After a period of socializing, then I can return again to what is often very lonely, creative work.* (L.C.)

ACTION 2: Think about the ways you like to take care of yourself after completing your creative project. Describe in your journal what you like to do at this time.

After you have completed a creative project, treat yourself to whatever you need to do to take care of yourself. Allow yourself to do whatever you need to do to rejuvenate yourself. And then you will be ready to start all over again, going through the same process toward your next creative act.

EVALUATION OF THE PROCESS

Before you begin again, we suggest you review your process, reminding yourself which parts were easy, which difficult. You can evaluate your engagement in the whole process. Use this downtime as an opportunity to consider your just completed work.

ACTION 3: Here you will take inventory of what you have learned from your latest creative project with the hopes of applying the lessons when you begin a new one. Write down your evaluations of your creative production.

What form of expression did you choose?
Was it satisfying? How?
Note what parts, keys, of the creative process were especially difficult for you.
What parts, keys, were easier for you?

ACTION 4: Write detailed answers that will help you next time with each of the following steps along the creative process. How did you deal with each of the steps? Which were easy? And which were more difficult for you? Where were your greatest obstacles? Where can you improve next time? How?

KEY 1: Getting Started on the Creative Process

_____
_____
_____
_____
_____

KEY 2: Making a Clearing for Your Creative Space

_____

_____

_____

_____

_____

KEY 3: Paying Attention to Inner and Outer Signals

_____

_____

_____

_____

_____

KEY 4: Staring into Space and Doing Nothing

_____

_____

_____

_____

_____

KEY 5: Finding Your Creative Direction

_____

_____

_____

_____

_____

Connecting to Creativity ~

KEY 6: Imagining the Creative Act

_____
_____
_____
_____
_____

KEY 7: Getting It out of Your Head

_____
_____
_____
_____
_____

KEY 8: Creating the Work

_____
_____
_____
_____
_____

KEY 9: Sharing Your Creation

_____
_____
_____
_____
_____

ACTION 5: Look back over the journal, or journals (or notes you may have written in this book), everything that you kept during the time of your past project. Here you can both review the process and re-discover other ideas you may have jotted down for future projects. Note your ideas that may help you as you prepare to enter another stage on the cycle of creative endeavor.

_____

_____

_____

_____

_____

BEGINNING AGAIN

If you have been excited by this process of creativity, then start the cycle over again with a new creation, and return to chapter 1. You may want to take classes in your chosen form of expression and learn more about your field of choice. Remember, too, that you can also change the form of your creative expression, but you will still need to begin at the beginning of the process.

This time it will be easier if you let yourself follow the natural steps described in this book.

~ *I have made some kind of art all my life. When I was a teenager, I wrote poetry, danced, tried to be a painter, played the piano. After school, my gang and I would all get together and play piano or make up skits. My growing up was a very creative time for me. There was no television so we all had to make our own fun. Now, after having made my career as a dancer, I have gone back to writing and visual expression through photography and sometimes I make up songs. I like to express myself in many ways, depending on how it feels to me that my expression wants to be made concrete. I feel I am always either starting a new project, dreaming of one, or in the middle of one. My life seems to need this for me to be complete.* (L.B.)

ACTION 6: List the actions you will now take to begin again.

_____

_____

_____

_____

In what direction do you think your creativity will go this time?
What must you do to get started again?
Begin again! You owe it to yourself and the world.
One day your heart starts pounding differently. Ideas come back into your brain. A focus begins to shape in your mind's eye. You begin to have fervor for life again. You wake up at dawn. You stay up all night until sunrise. You are not available to anyone. You have shot off like a cannon, and there is no stopping you. It might last an hour; it might last a week or more. You feel as if you are on fire—you know you are glowing. You feel your purpose—you feel at one with the universe. You are in the grip of the universal flow, and you cannot let loose. It feels God-given—it is a charged feeling like no other. It is the ecstasy of creation. You are beginning again the creative process.

RE-COMMITTING TO THE CREATIVE PROCESS

Living in a culture that often does not appreciate creative people and their endeavors, it is important to re-commit on a regular basis to fulfilling your creative potential. At least once a year, perhaps on your birthday or the anniversary of your starting another major creative project, you will want to review the year's creative activities and re-commit yourself to another year to come. Commitment to fulfilling your creative potential is not ever a one-time action. You must re-commit yourself over and over throughout your life.

~ *Throughout the year, I have different anniversaries to commemorate that have to do with moments of great creativity in my life. I always dedicate some time on those days to going off alone to think about those occasions and what they have meant for me. And, usually, for private remembrance of very special creative days, I try to spend the whole day alone contemplating its meaning and how I can use the memory to inspire my future work and life.* (L.C.)

ACTION 7: Describe what you will do to symbolize your re-committal to your creative process and to the fulfillment of your creative potential.

_____

_____

_____

_____

THE JOYS OF CREATION

You have now found that expressing part of yourself through the creative process is one of the most fulfilling experiences of your life. We hope that you have discovered the joy of creation—that it has given you some of the most ecstatic moments in your life. Whatever the trials, whatever the pitfalls—and most creative people will acknowledge that the creative process can also be torturous—there is no experience like it on this earth. It is still compelling and wonderful. Often artists have been called driven, impassioned, and out of control in their need to express themselves or to create their work.

This sometimes lonely adventure is clearly worth it when the highs of the moment of creation are experienced. It does not always have to be lonely. It can be equally exhilarating to work collaboratively—after each collaborator has done her/his own individual immersion in the creative process—a topic we will discuss in our next book.

We hope that you have had such an exhilarating experience in this process, the experience of touching something miraculous and something so fulfilling that no other experience can approach it.

We hope you will continue in your quest for this experience throughout your life.

We wish you every success in this endeavor.

We are all participants in this creative process.

NEVER FORGET:

You are unique, and
  No one else can think what you think
  Dream what you dream
  Sing what you sing
  Say what you say
  CREATE WHAT YOU CREATE.

Keys

⤳ *Expressing part of yourself through the creative process is one of the most fufilling experiences of your life.*

⤳ *Whatever the trials, whatever the pitfalls, there is no other experience like completing a creative work.*

⤳ *Beginning again, from the beginning, is always part of the creative process, and each time you must do it—begin all over again.*

⤳ *You must re-commit to fulfilling your creative potential and the creative process.*

ABOUT THE AUTHORS

~~~~~~

ELIZABETH WEIL BERGMANN is an award-winning Juilliard-trained dancer and choreographer who, in responding to her creative voices, has also become a poet and photographer. She holds a Master of Arts degree in Dance Education from the University of Michigan, where she established the university's Department of Dance. Later she developed the Dance Department at Shenandoah University. Currently professor and director of dance at Florida International University in Miami, Liz Bergmann recently served as a Fulbright Senior Scholar in Trinidad and is also a choreographer in the Caribbean.

ELIZABETH OVERTON COLTON is a prize-winning international journalist and Emmy Award–winning television producer, and is also a novelist and nonfiction author. A graduate of Randolph-Macon Woman's College, she holds Master's degrees from Vanderbilt University and a doctorate in social anthropology from the London School of Economics. Professor of Mass Communication at Shenandoah University, Fulbright-awardee, and former MacArthur Fellow with the Globalization Project of the University of Chicago, Liz Colton is currently serving as a Knight International Press Fellow with the International Center for Journalists.

Bergmann and Colton conduct workshops and seminars on the creative process around the world.

Lucha Corpi was born in Jáltipan, Veracruz, in 1945, and moved with her family to San Luis Potosí when she was nine. At the age of nineteen she married and came to live and study in Berkeley. She holds a B.A. from the University of California, Berkeley, and an M.A. from San Francisco State University, in Comparative Literature. Her poems have appeared in many literary magazines and anthologies. The first collection was published in *Fireflight: Three Latin American Poets* (Berkeley: Oyez, 1976). In 1979 Ms. Corpi was the recipient of a full fellowship for creative writing, awarded by the National Endowment for the Arts. She lives in Oakland, California, where she teaches English as a Second Language in the Oakland Public Schools Neighborhood Centers.

Catherine Rodríguez-Nieto was born in Minot, North Dakota, in 1937. She holds a B.A. in Spanish and English from the College of St. Catherine in St. Paul, Minnesota, and an M.A. in Spanish from the University of California, Berkeley. She was a Smith-Mundt Scholar in Panama, and an *Assistante d'anglais* in Toulouse, France. Her translations have appeared in several anthologies and literary magazines. *Fireflight: Three Latin American Poets* was her first book of translations. She and her husband live in Oakland, California, with their two children. They are the owners of a translation and editing service in Berkeley, *In Other Words . . . Inc.*

Total Recall

One day I'll wake up
and I'll have forgotten everything
My eyes will search the whiteness
not realizing that they themselves are snow
I'll be everywhere
because I'll be nowhere
with all of time between my hands
and no more space
than what hangs suspended
between death and oblivion

Then I'll know everything